Rental Property Investing

Unlock the Secrets of Real Estate Investing and Management, Including Tips on Negotiation and Finding Investment Properties that Will Give You Passive Long-term Income

Contents

Introduction

When it comes to real estate investment properties, the first thing that might pop into your mind is your home; however, *residential real estate* can play a significant role in any successful and diversified portfolio.

When you invest in residential real estate—most often referred to as leased property, and is a tangible asset—you get a secure and interactive investment opportunity that enables you to expand your financial portfolio. Furthermore, having a rental property is a safe and excellent means to grow your wealth.

Rental property investment and management can be as simple as playing a game of monopoly, as long as you master the fundamental factors of economics, finance, and risk. To succeed, you have to purchase properties, avoid bankruptcy, and generate rent so that you can buy more properties. But don't forget that "simple" doesn't mean "easy". If you make a mistake, the results can span from minor to major disasters. You may even find yourself broke or worse.

In this book, you will learn the secrets that successful investors use to run their property investments.

The first chapter details the basics and responsibilities of becoming a landlord.

Next, you will learn how to find investment properties that can provide both short-term and long-term rental income. Once you have mastered the different strategies, you will then learn how to run the actual property.

Following on from this, you will discover how to add value to your rental property, including how to build a successful business model.

The fourth and fifth chapters focus on how to analyze your rental property and the different ways you can finance your property, respectively.

The sixth chapter delves into the best methods to negotiate deals. You will learn why listening is critical when you need to start a negotiation, and why you should use mirrors in your conversation.

The final chapter concentrates on the *best* secrets of rental property investing and management. Most importantly, how to choose the right plan, how to select members for your rental investment team, and how to manage your rentals and exit strategies.

Lastly, you will learn about the mistakes to avoid in rental property investment.

Whether you are new to rental property investing or organizing your third income property, this book has great nuggets of advice.

Time to dive in!

Chapter 1: Becoming a Landlord

Becoming a landlord can be a great option for increasing your wealth. If this is your plan, here are some solid first-time pointers:

- Be ready for the kind of work involved. From screening for tenants to filling out legal agreements to taking care of utilities, it is crucial to know what you are getting yourself into.

- As a landlord, you need a real estate lawyer to assist you in dealing with any legal problems that might occur. Different federal and state laws deal with rental matters, such as security deposits, lease agreements, discrimination, late rental payments, and maintenance.

- If you own a property that you would like to rent out, but you don't want to deal with the everyday tasks, then look for a property management company.

- You will need to work hard to get the right tenants. If your tenants turn out to be bad choices, then you need to be ready to evict them.

Own a Rental Home: The Journey to Wealth

According to a report by the National Association of Realtor's 2017 Investment and Vacation Home Buyers Survey, in 2016, investment property increased from 1.09 million to 1.14 million.

Working as a landlord can take different forms. You can be entirely free, allowing others to do all the work for you, or you can be your own boss and gradually grow your net worth. However, it is not for everyone.

Do you have the skills and experience it takes?

Only a few newbies find it easy to become a landlord. For many, it is just hard work. Some experience problems, especially when the economy and market aren't running well—that is when tenants begin to fail to pay the rent.

If you have lived in a rented house or apartment, you may have never met your landlord. That is because he or she may have chosen to let other people maintain and manage the property.

Alternatively, your landlord may have lived in one of the rooms in your building. So you may have met or passed each other every day without knowing. Or they may have done all tasks and responsibilities like repairing a leaky faucet.

The Primary Tasks of a Landlord

Whether landlords decide to do everything on their own or appoint others to do it, they still have the primary responsibility for many tasks, such as:

Finding the right tenants

1. Advertising for new tenants – You'll soon learn how to get in touch with your target market. However, today's online platform provides local classified advertising, like Craigslist, that is considered cost-effective.

2. Filing legal agreements – You need to have a lease agreement for every rental. Crucial items to include in a lease are clear statements that show who is responsible for different tasks, such as maintaining of the yard to ensure upkeep of appliances.

3. You can let your attorney create one, or you could build yours on a template from a certified website.

4. Disclosing the home to potential clients – This is generally a sales chance that can help reduce the dead time that occurs between tenants. However, this is a chance to clear away potential clients that don't qualify.

5. Vet renters to avoid vandals and deadbeats – Different companies, some on the internet, provide credit and verification checks to the landlord.

Managing your property

1. Collecting rent and deposits – Don't forget this!

2. Set and enforce rules – The most successful landlords like to implement rules rigidly. Tenants have no option but to abide by the rules and regulations.

3. Solving insurance and liability issues – These may include swimming pools, icy paths, and ensuring that the home is up to standard.

4. Maintaining books and monitoring tax write-offs – Ensure that you can claim all the deductions created for you.

5. Observing local landlord-tenant laws – The only worse thing than being in court is losing in court.

6. Maintain the correct records for legal and tax purposes – You never know when the court and IRS will ask you for such details.

It is good to try out only those tasks and responsibilities for which you believe you have the time and skills. However, the work that you outsource will cost you and reduce the gains of your venture.

Accidental rental or professional aspiration?

Some people are born into being a landlord, attain the position, or have it thrust upon them. This means they either inherit a rental property, purchase it, or become landlords unexpectedly.

Those who become a landlord by accident are usually homeowners who had to move to a different location, probably for family reasons or work, but could not sell their house. This could have been because they had "negative equity" or the local property market was poor, and nobody was buying. Hence, to ensure they have money, they had to rent out the original home.

Tenant-proofing

This is usually good for the renter because the tenant gets to live in a homeowner's "pride and joy". However, if the tenant doesn't take good care of the home, as well as the owner, that can easily change. The "pride and joy" may quickly turn into a pigsty.

To deal with this risk, some landlords "tenant-proof" their properties. It could mean repairing destroyed hardwood flooring using inexpensive carpets and linoleum, while also removing weak aspects that may have been abused, such as a wood stove.

That said, tenant-proofing should be considered in the form of content marketing. If you want to attract high-end renters that will pay for quality services, then they need some luxury. If people in your target market are interested in a roof over their heads, your goal should be to secure the value of your asset.

Professional help

As a landlord, some people think that they can do all the above tasks by themselves. Although some succeed, many people don't find enough time in a day, especially when they have another job. They may also lack the skills to perform all the necessary maintenance and repair work.

Thus, they decide to look for a professional to assist them. The few who may not have the time to choose, go for a full-time service property management company, which will manage all tasks on their behalf. The costs for property management depend on the current local market, the task that they want to avoid, and whether the rental is short or long term.

In the US, the long-term rental management falls in the range of 8-15%. However, the short-term properties in the resort areas may cost more than 50% to manage. Every week, the place will need to be cleaned, reservations taken, lines replaced, and rent collected.

Select from the menu

This can cause the full-service plan to become very expensive for many landlords. So they look at the list of tasks as a menu, and then they select things that they can personally do well and outsource the rest.

Those who are good around the house pick the routine repair tasks, and the ones with genuine construction experience can take on all kinds of labor a home may require. Similarly, some may be very strong at administrative duties or have excellent people skills. The right thing is to play to your strengths when choosing tasks that you want to do.

Don't risk chances

The golden rule has always been not to pretend that you are good at things when you aren't. Don't fret or feel bad about your limitations; everyone has them.

Some people just aren't meant to wield a tool or find that their eyes get tired reading a legal document. Others are natural accountants or can be more sympathetic regarding a tenant who is behind in their rent or approaching a breach of their lease.

So you always need to remember the old saying, "Don't trip over dollars to pick up pennies." In other words, don't ruin your business to save a few dollars, especially when you have doubts about legal problems. It is better to hire an attorney.

What about being a landlord anonymously?

If you live in one of the rooms in the building you own, you may experience some advantages. Nobody can look after your biggest asset better than you. Besides that, your commute time will be short.

However, living on the premises has its challenges. To start, there is a need for some emotional distance from your tenants. If you become friends with them, it may become difficult to avoid their pleas if they ever pay the rent late. Additionally, they may convince you not to follow all the rules or frequently subject you to their complaints.

If you don't want people to knock at your door all the time to complain about minor issues, then you should live away from the property.

One way that you can overcome this is by not disclosing to those around you that you are the owner; instead, you can use a property manager to run the building.

Chapter 2: Finding Investment Properties

When it comes to rental property investing, you are perhaps wondering which types of rental properties you should invest your money in. Well, the answer is simple: different types of rental properties fulfill the needs of various real estate investors. Every kind of rental property investment has its advantages and drawbacks, including return on investment, cash on return, the frequency of cash flows, and other factors. That said, what are the best types of real estate properties for investing?

Long-Term Versus Short-Term Rental Properties

As a rental property investor, it is good to set your investing goals before starting to browse through different types of properties. The decision of whether to go for the long-term or short-term rental strategies depends on the finance method you choose and the location of the property. If you select the long-term rental plan, you ensure a continuous flow of income that will pay your mortgage bills. However, this is not the case with short-term rentals, where the location is critical in defining the rate of occupancy of your property.

For that reason, long-term rental properties are the most popular type of rental property in real estate investing. Long-term rentals are rented out for at least six months and are chosen among new and experienced real estate investors since they provide a steady income that will pay off the investment, increase in value over time, and can be used against home equity loans.

The significant risk that long-term rental properties pose is a vacancy, and this can be eliminated by investing in a property located in the best location that will fulfill the needs of the tenants; for example, investing in single-family homes that are close to schools. Another drawback that comes with long-term rental properties is handling tenants. Becoming a landlord is not a simple job, especially if you have stubborn and demanding tenants. That is why hiring a property management firm can spare you the everyday issues and relieve you of the stress—but they come at a cost.

On the other hand, short-term rentals work on a nightly basis. In other words, the time interval of when a tenant can stay ranges between one night and six months. Property owners can rent out their homes or even purchase investment properties for the sole purpose of renting them out on a short-term basis. Some of the companies that facilitate short-term rentals include HomeAway, Airbnb, VRBO, and others. The main advantage of having a short rental property, especially in a strategic location, is the vast profits generated compared to renting the same property for an extended period. However, because of the level of competition in this business, landlords have to set up a competitive advantage to maintain occupancy rates.

Types of Rental Properties

Normal apartment

An apartment is a rented living space within a residential building that may have one or more rooms, which is good for a person or family. It is possible to have different apartment units in a single residential complex, but every apartment is self-contained and can be owned or rented.

An apartment should contain all the necessary rooms that an individual will require, such as a bathroom, kitchen, bedroom, and amenities. But some apartments have other features. Take, for example, a studio apartment; this is best for one person because it has just one room that acts as a living, dining, and bedroom, with a small kitchen and bathroom.

A garden apartment is often surrounded by a landscaped area, similar to a townhouse, while a loft apartment has different units housed within a multi-story building. The definition may appear blurry, with other types of flats present today, but most of the apartment units are ideal for an individual or small family.

Serviced apartments

A serviced apartment is a top-end rental property that has all the necessary amenities of an average apartment but also offers other services. That means that it has a scheduled cleaning service, maid services, repairs, and other perks that you can find at a restaurant or hotel. This apartment is best suited for individuals that want something additional from the deal, better space, privacy, and an extended stay. The purpose of a serviced apartment is to offer one of the best luxurious spaces to ensure that the tenant feels at home. Like most apartments, a serviced apartment also has private spaces and common spaces for all the occupants.

Street house/detached house

A detached house is a free-standing building different from a normal family-owned house with a private parking area, patio, and garden. The house can be a single story or multiple stories, with other functions such as boundary fences, a pool, a garage, and a driveway. This is a bit different from a row house or street house that is built side by side with other units. The row house can be a multi-story complex similar to an apartment, but they often contain more floor space and the lowest level can be occupied by shops and offices. A row house can also resemble an apartment complex, but the latter usually have a shared space, and the building has elevators, staircases, and pathways for everyone. Unlike houses, the apartments are furnished with appliances and furniture by the landlord.

Bed and Breakfast

Shortened as "BnB", this is a private home designed for guests to stay overnight. As the name suggests, it has an inclusive breakfast and other social amenities. Bed and breakfasts exist in all different types and are unique depending on the region and city. They generally have a better value than other facilities.

Bungalow

A bungalow is a low home featuring a large front porch without an upper floor or upper rooms set in the roof. Bungalow homes offer easy mobility for the elderly, disabled, or children because there is just one floor. A bungalow has lots of charm because of the different types of homes that were built in the early 1900s.

Condominium

Also known as a "condo", this refers to a building or a complex of buildings that have individually-owned apartments. Most condos provide more amenities than apartments.

Cottage

A cottage is generally a small home, typically one story. Cottages are constructed in a wide range of materials that comprise of stone, wattle, or wood. Cottages are cozy and are common in rural or semi-rural regions.

Hostel

This is a low-budget accommodation used among travelers. When a person books a stay in a hostel, they are typically booking for a single night, but not the whole room. A bed can be in a room shared with four to twenty travelers at a time. Bathrooms in a hostel are dorm style, with different shower stalls and a row of sinks. Hostels are cheap and provide an individual the chance to interact with different kinds of people; however, they don't offer the convenience and comfort of a hotel.

Mansion

A large, expensive, and beautiful house.

Townhome

By definition, a townhouse is a tall, narrow, and traditional row house that has three or more floors. Because of the close distance to neighbors and shared walls, this may result in noise and limited privacy. Despite that, a townhome is furnished with great amenities, such as playgrounds, swimming pools, tennis courts, clubhouses, and much more.

Villa

Historically, villas were considered an upper-class country estate constructed by Romans. Nowadays, things have changed because they have been redesigned into semi-detached homes in a residential district.

Chalet

Chalets resemble cabins; the only exception is that they have paneled sides and angled roofs. Chalets are generally connected with mountain and hillside vistas. They are luxurious and come equipped with Jacuzzis and fireplaces. Also, they have spacious decks and verandas. Other great amenities, such as Wi-Fi, water, and electricity, are included too.

The Best Types of Rental Properties for Investing

Now that you are familiar with the different types of rental properties let's look at the ones that you can invest in.

Single-family homes

These are detached structures that usually house a single family. You will often see them in suburban areas because the land prices are much lower than in urban. After assessing all types of rental properties, single-family homes are perhaps the best for different reasons:

- *High demand:* Even when the housing market records losses, you'll always see a demand for single-family homes.

- *Affordable investments*: If you compare them with other types of rental properties, single-family homes require the least amount of capital for investment.

- *Simple to finance:* As long as you have a down payment of at least 20% of the buying price, mortgage lenders are willing to fund your rental investment.

A drawback of investing in single family homes, however, is that you have to be ready to perform all the responsibilities of a landlord. Although you can decide to hire a property management company, that is not the best thing to do.

Multi-family homes

A multi-family home is a residential property that contains a minimum of two housing units. What makes these types of rental properties exciting for investment is the massive cash flow they generate. However, the process of financing these homes is more complicated than single-family homes. Not only are they costly, but also it is not easy to qualify for a residential real estate loan. Lastly, the multi-family home has to have four units or less.

Townhouses

These are very common in urban areas. Townhouses are defined by their small square footage area per floor on multiple floors. In general, townhouses are cheaper compared to single-family homes because the demand is higher for the latter.

The Bottom Line

When it comes to rental property investing, it is hard to choose which of the different types of real estate properties is the best. It all depends on the prices of houses in your given area, your readiness to become a landlord, and your financing goals.

Types of Property That Can Be Used as Short-Term Rentals

How can a newbie in real estate investing choose the best types of properties to turn into rental properties, especially when they have a short-term rental investment strategy?

In this section, we look at some of the most popular rental properties that you can turn into short-term rentals and make a good income.

The types of properties differ from one another in terms of the season, location, general year performance, maintenance, and running costs. The aim is to give you a better idea of what you need to expect when factoring in the different types of properties to choose from.

There is a wide variety of rental properties that are being used as short-term rentals in real estate investing; however, experienced rental property investors know that all types of properties are the same. For every rental property, there is a different method of management to fulfill the objective as an income generating asset.

Among all the different rental property types that can be changed into a short-term rental, these are the most popular in today's real estate market. They have pros and cons and qualities that make them unique from other forms of rental properties:

Seasonal vacation rentals

Vacation rentals are the most common type of properties that rental property investors buy. This is because the rentals are straightforward in performance, and they almost guarantee profits during specific times of the year.

Investing in a vacation rental has different advantages, but the most evident advantage and the reason why they are so popular among millennials is the duality of their performance.

Although experienced and long-time investors may prefer to invest in properties that will create the highest returns, millennials like properties that they can make profits from, and which will allow them to save money and use it for other purposes.

Vacation rentals can save money by acting as an accommodation for the owner in case they choose to travel to a place to enjoy time with their family. This provides the owners of the vacation rentals with a means for making extra income and a secondary home that they can use whenever they want.

Also, vacation rentals are found in locations that have the highest number of travelers and tourists, especially during summer. If you are searching for a vacation rental to buy and turn into a short-term rental, you need to ensure that you choose a location that you would want to go on a vacation to.

The major disadvantage that comes with vacation rentals is their seasonality. This implies that even though vacation rentals may perform well during the high season, the performance will drop in the other months of the year, and you may struggle to make profits when you enter the low seasons.

This also means that you if you decide to live in the property during the high season, you will be significantly reducing the amount of money you can earn from the property, so make sure that you make arrangements with your finances in the best way possible.

Luxury Homes

Luxury homes are not the most popular type of short-term rentals, especially for beginner rental estate investors. The reason for this is that luxury homes will generally require a fortune as an investment. Not only are these homes costly to buy, but also their maintenance and management costs are *very* high.

However, if you are a creative individual, have confidence in your advertising and marketing abilities, and have sufficient money to buy the property, then luxury homes can be quite profitable.

Generally, you shouldn't expect to rent out your luxury home regularly during the year. However, when you finally rent it out, you should expect to receive a lot of money from it. Remember that the people who want to rent a luxury home are those with tons of money, and they are ready to pay extra if you provide them with a premium stay and pleasant experience.

As a result, individuals who own luxury homes will often look for a top-notch property management company that offers exceptional experience during the period of the tenant's stay, attempts to convert each tenant into a potential customer, and gets them to suggest your property to their friends. This is the point where the success of luxury homes can start or fail.

Just keep in mind, though, that luxury homes are a big gamble, and losing money on your investment may not give you another chance to invest in any other property in the future.

Gateway Homes

These properties are located in remote locations or in areas that are far away from the cities. Gateway homes are commonly used by people who want to detach from the busy life of the city and enjoy quiet and restful times in nature.

Although this may not be something that you are targeting, many people are searching for this type of rental property.

There are several factors that you need to remember before you invest in gateway homes as short-term rentals:

- Gateway homes are cheap to buy and cheap to rent. Therefore, you should not put too much expectation on the amount of rental income you can generate from them.

- Don't expect to spend much money on the maintenance and management of these properties. Since the homes are built using wood materials and are small in size, any form of repairs or maintenance that is required will be minimal.

- Tenants that want to move into a gateway home will usually rent it for some months, which is longer than the period for other short-term rentals. In other words, gateway homes are middle-term rentals.

- In general, you shouldn't experience any legal problems when renting out a gateway home because most legal issues with short-term rentals occur with hotels and other forms of accommodation.

- Examples of gateway homes include bungalows, cabins, cottages, and chalets.

Gateway homes are special rental properties that you can choose to invest in, and most real estate investors recommend them to beginner investors because they are cheap investments with low levels of risk.

With the many different types of rental properties that are available to invest in, newbies can sometimes struggle to identify the one that fits their investment goals and personality.

How to Choose Your First Rental Property

Renting a real estate property is considered one of the best methods to build personal wealth. According to real estate investors owning dozens of rental properties, one can make a massive annual profit at the same time as building wealth in the equity of their properties. For one to attain this level of success, it is important to make the first step and buy your first rental property. In most cases, the first property in rental portfolios is the most important because its failure or success will usually define whether or not an investor commits so much to real estate. Below are some tips to help you choose your first rental property to ensure that it is a success:

1. Set your parameters

The first thing in choosing a rental property is identifying several basic features of what you are looking for. Determine, for example, the location you want the rental to be in. Cities and neighborhoods around colleges or near business centers will provide decent high rental income. Besides that, you have to decide the type of property you want to buy. In the previous section, we looked at the different types of rental properties that investors can purchase. Most investors prefer single-family homes; however, some may be interested in the idea of a duplex property that can generate multiple rental incomes. These types of properties also have the advantage of generating income even if a single tenant moves out.

The amount of money in your bank account is another vital factor to consider. Most beginner investors tend to believe that the more money they spend, the more profit they will make. Although this may be true on certain levels, it is also possible to make good profits from a lower-cost property, especially when it is in the right location and attracts the right tenants. Decide on the amount of money you are willing to spend or borrow to invest and try to stick to that figure as you look for properties.

2. Create a list of the best properties

Once you have made up your mind on what you are looking for in a property, it is time to search your local area for homes that suit your criteria. Look in neighborhood areas that you think are good to own rental property for homes that are near your price range. Make sure that you factor in the size, condition, and age of the property. Also take into account any other factors that may affect how much you would charge in rent. Online listings can be handy at this stage because they will list square footage, bathrooms, bedrooms, and pertinent utility information. Besides this, they will also show inside pictures of the home, which you can use to assess the general condition.

Although the number of properties that you'll see will vary depending on the availability in the market and the criteria you select, you should target finding a minimum of ten properties that are worth further investigation. Even if you feel like you are lucky to get your perfect property on your first or second attempt, keep looking for others. When you have a long list of candidates, it gives you more options and increases the chances of settling on a property that fulfills your criteria.

Here is an example of the criteria you may use:

- At least three bedrooms

- A minimum of 1.5 bathrooms

- At least 900 square feet

- The minimum year built: 1991

- The minimum monthly rent: $900/month

- The renovation budget should not be more than the cost of the home

- One-car garage

- The target buying price: $45,000-$105,000

Narrow down the list

Next, you need to organize the display for each of the homes so that you can accurately see inside. This step alone will naturally narrow down your list because there are some properties that you will decide don't suit your standards. For the remaining properties, you need to conduct in-depth research. Look for rental listings for similar properties in the nearby neighborhood to identify the standard of rent. Start to compare each property's possible rental income to its price, and you'll soon be left with just two or three properties that offer the highest possible return on investment.

Look for more financing options

Now that you have done the hardest part of choosing a handful of great properties, it is time to determine your financing power. In most cases, this will not differ too much from property to property because most investment demands that you take out a mortgage. However, you will often get lucky and find a property that the current owner will be ready to finance at a more affordable rate than what a bank would offer. If this happens with one of the properties on your list, it could tip the balance in favor of the property.

Take action

So far, every step that we have looked at in choosing your first rental property is free. Many people who start in rental property investment reach this point and stop. If you want to realize success in rental investment, you will need to buy a property at some point. Choose the property you think is the best investment and start the process by purchasing it. If you believe you may have missed other opportunities or you just don't see the properties that you are left with as being as attractive as you had expected, it is okay to begin to look for other options. However, ensure that you proceed with the intention of purchasing a property as soon as possible.

The process of starting in rental property investment to becoming a successful investor is a long one. If you can apply an elaborate selection process on your first property, you can prepare yourself to invest wisely and succeed. Make sure that you always pick the best available properties, and you'll more likely experience success as an investor.

Finding Investment Properties for Sale – Personal Investor Networks

Rental property investment involves doing business with people. The relationships that a real estate investor builds throughout his or her career are critical. It is possible that a person you know well is aware of a great deal or can connect you with someone who knows one. Networking is considered the best way to identify rental properties for sale that are known to a few people. Furthermore, in this way, an investor can purchase the property at a lower price.

A survey conducted by 12,000 business professionals in the Business Networking International group clarified why networking is essential. From this survey, the study found that people who spent an average of 6.3 hours of networking per week boosted their success in business.

However, people who spent less than two hours per week networking did not benefit much from it at all. This study demonstrated that the more time a person devotes to networking, the higher the level of success he or she is likely to receive.

One of the most exciting things that emerged from this survey is that out of 12,000 participants, men spent MORE time networking than women, but generated a lower percent from business referrals than women. Does it mean that women are better networkers?

Well, perhaps, and there seems to be a good reason for this.

Men like to be more formal and transaction-oriented when networking. It is known as "cut to the chase networking", and it is not as effective as the kind of networking women do.

While it is not true in every instance, most often men love to talk about business first and personal issues afterward. On the other hand, women do the opposite.

In most cases, when men try to focus on the relationship first approach, the approach appears forced. Then because of that awkward feeling, they get on to business talk because it is easy and safe to discuss.

This study demonstrated that women tend to be better with plain small talk and becoming personal without appearing too personal or forced. When you become natural and easy in your approach, people tend to like you better and respond in a friendly manner. But men often stiffen up at this stage.

The following focuses on how the "relationship first" is a significant factor, and it doesn't matter whether you are a man or woman; we can all get better at it.

The participants in the study who attributed their success through networking felt that the best way is to build a relationship first, then concentrate on the business after that.

The more you concentrate on getting to know the other person and understanding them emotionally, without disrespecting them, the better you increase the odds of networking.

Networking is the best way to identify suitable investment properties for sale that aren't known to every real estate investor. Some user groups that you can network include:

> • **Personal Investor Network:** This may comprise of landlords that you've met that have investment properties or even an old friend who works as a rental investor.

• **Investment Clubs:** These are great places to find rental properties. Usually, you'll see an email list where every member of the club promotes properties for sale. If you haven't joined any yet, you should do it fast.

• **Real Estate Investor Meetups:** These are the most accessible groups for a person to join. For instance, Meetup.com is an excellent place to find networks for investors. Just search for "real estate investing", and several groups will show up. Attend different meetups, get the relevant contacts, and begin to grow your network.

• **Personal Acquaintances:** The people you see in a rental investment industry aren't the only people that can assist you in finding rental investment property deals. Even your family friends can help you find prospective investment properties for sale. These people may have their networks who are aware of great rental property investment opportunities.

How to become a better networker?

In most cases, you may find it hard to create a relationship while at these "networking events". By going to Business Networking International meetings, Chambers of Commerce meetings, and Rotary Club events, you increase your chances of meeting people and getting to know them.

However, the actual relationship takes place when you remove that card and reach out to the person and invite them to have a coffee, breakfast, or lunch. This way, your relationship has the best opportunity of going to the next level.

The trust and goodwill you develop by knowing them on an individual level is the "social capital" that improves a mutually rewarding kind of business relationship.

Now, if you think that networking has not played a role in your business success, you are likely doing either one or both of these things wrong:

- *You haven't given it enough time*: In general, six-plus hours per week is a good starting point.

- *You aren't doing it correctly:* That means that you are possibly going for the "business first" instead of the "relationship first".

Ensure that every hour you spend is an hour well spent—whether it is going to meet new real estate investors for a joint venture, Internet marketing individuals, real estate brokers, home inspectors or private money lenders.

Keep in mind that networking is the way you grow your real estate investing business, and it all begins with building these types of relationships through networking.

Networking should be part of your marketing strategy

Don't consider it as a chore that you need to do. Just think of networking as part of your marketing strategy. The more time you dedicate to it, the better you become. Focus on being relational rather than business oriented.

Sometimes the best contacts you meet are the ones that you don't talk business with until the end of the conversation when you hear, "Oh, by the way, what is it that you do?" If you have arrived at this stage, where you have a strong, personal relationship before you talk about business, then you are perhaps on the right track. The chances are that a good personal relationship will emerge from the conversation as well as a mutually helpful business relationship.

So, take the next step and search around your area for networking opportunities, such as Chamber of Commerce networking insights, meetup.com, BNI groups, or local REIA meetings. You don't need to join all these networks; sign up for a few to get your feet wet. Set aside a certain percent of your time to physically attend these events every week. Then, once you arrive there, concentrate on being personal and relational—not in a business mindset. Get to know most people; then you can talk about business. Everyone in these groups is there for the same reason, so the business talk usually comes naturally. That is why you should never force it but allow it to develop on its own.

Once you have done this, you'll begin to see some differences in your real estate investing business. It will start to grow… and you didn't have to pay a marketing company $50,000 to do it for you.

That said, it is good to make your intentions known to members in your inner circle. They should know that you are looking for a property to buy. This way, you increase your chance of finding the best deals. Plus, it is possible that a coworker may be aware of someone wanting to sell.

Finding Investment Properties for Sale Online

Since the advent of technology, finding a real estate property has become easier. Several online websites are designed to facilitate the identification of rental properties for sale for investors. These sites have different resources, such as neighborhood information and records about the property.

The most popular websites designed to help you perform a property search are Realtor.com and Craigslist:

- **Craigslist.org.** More than a million people use Craigslist for different tasks and activities, and looking for a property on this platform is straightforward. First, you need to go the region of the nation you want, and then navigate to the "Real Estate for Sale" section to find out if there is a type of property that you consider attractive. Also, you can set your search criteria by entering the search words in the search box.

- **Realtor.com.** This site belongs to the National Association of Realtors' official site. This site grants you the ability to scan through millions of properties from different countries. The choice is yours if you want to browse through foreclosures. An excellent feature of Realtor.com is that it has a street address that one can use to narrow down their search. Again, you can register for the "search Assist" option so that you can receive an updated listing of rental properties. Realtors can be very useful while searching for investment properties for sale in different ways:

- Property investors can engage real estate agents for listings of properties which they have seen online.

- Property investors can talk to real estate offices, especially realtors, that are located in specific towns to find out about possible investment properties for sale.

- In certain offices, the real estate agents won't market some property listings on the Multiple Listing Services (MLS). Instead, they will send these property listings to their contacts. Therefore, a real estate investor has to be in the realtor's database to stay updated with the latest news on investment properties.

Finding Investment Properties for Sale – Print Media

Another efficient method used to identify investment properties is print media. Several investment properties are not advertised online; this means that there is low competition for them, which is a good thing for a property investor.

- *Newspapers.* If you are looking for properties that are sold by their owners, newspapers are a great bet.

- *Local Publications:* Properties can be found in these because realtor offices like to promote their listings in such publications.

Finding Investment Properties for Sale – Auctions

Of late, real estate auctions have become popular, especially for rental property investors who are searching for a bargain. Experienced real estate investors often find properties for sale using this method, and keep in mind that technology has made everything easier and enjoyable for new investors.

Even though you can get different types of rental investment properties at an auction, the majority are foreclosures. Auctions comprise two categories: online and live. The online method is increasingly becoming popular as property investors feel secure to make online purchases. A real estate investor can look for properties for sale on auction websites like auction.com.

Finding Investment Properties for Sale through MLS

The Multiple Listing Service (MLS) is mostly used by a specific group of rental property investors. The major function is allowing the investor to access accurate and organized information about investment properties.

For quite some time, this has been the source of rental investment property transactions. The reason is that it has major exposure to seller brokers, and delivers many different choices to buyer brokers.

Besides this, the database listing of MLS is one of the most accurate on the internet. Since it is free to access information on its database, there is high competition—if you choose to use it.

Regardless of the choice you make, always remember that the process of buying an investment property can be challenging. Despite this, it is wise to know the different sources in which you can find real estate investment properties. Why? The next deal may emerge from any place.

Factors to pay attention to when buying an investment rental property

While it is possible to generate income from real estate investing, there is more to it than buying the first house. Keep in mind that TV programs about investing in rental properties paint a reality that is far from what happens in real life. If you are considering buying a rental investment property, ensure that you read these factors first:

1. The state of the house

There's no problem with choosing to buy a fixer-upper, but you need to be realistic about the money and time that you'll spend on making it look beautiful.

Once you receive a detailed inspection report from a certified professional, you next have to ask yourself the number of repairs that you can do by yourself and count the number of repairs that may require external contractors. Find estimates for any big task that you may need to conduct.

You'll have to confirm that critical problems are fixed before someone comes in, keeping in mind that no one will want to live in an unsafe house. Also, it may result in severe consequences if tenants get sick or hurt.

Determine the time that the repairs may take. For example, if the house needs to remain vacant for some months, this may not be the right property to choose.

2. Follow the 1% Rule

Investors have their principles that guide them on how to use profits, but many of them will tell you that the profit you make has to respect the 1% rule.

For instance, when you buy a house for $100,000, it would need to generate $1,000 every month. This amount is arrived at by doing a simple calculation:

Take the estimated monthly rent and divide it by the price of the house. ($1,000/$100,000=1%).

You should only attempt to buy a house that doesn't fulfill the 1% rule if the property is located in a neighborhood that is quickly changing with the value of rents and homes expected to increase over the short period.

3. Insurance costs

If you aren't careful, insurance can consume all your gains, and that is why you need to have done thorough research. First, you must choose the type of coverage for your investment property. Decide whether you would like to pay a little each month, but get a big cut when you make a claim, and whether you are going to cover your tenants or not.

Next, decide whether the area you're interested in has high insurance premiums as a result of its vulnerability to tornadoes, earthquakes, floods, and other natural disasters. If so, the house may not be worth it.

When you think you are ready, compare different rates.

4. Property taxes

If you plan to buy an investment property, then you must always consider property taxes. If you have a high tax, you'll realize that the taxes will consume most of your profit. However, if you have to pay low taxes, at least a significant amount of profit that you earn will remain.

One thing that you should always remember is that property taxes are higher in metropolitan regions and lower in rural places. Charges will differ depending on the area; that is why you should solicit a local tax professional to help you understand the rate of taxes.

5. Neighborhood

Just like the condition of the house is essential, the location also commands the same importance. You have to pick an area wisely and ensure that it's an area the tenant will enjoy.

The most critical thing to look at is safety. Make sure that the crime rate isn't too high. Curb appeal is another important factor because many tenants want to live on a street that has nicely painted homes.

If you are considering renting your property to a family, you may have to look for places that are near a school district. Parents will be more willing to rent properties that are close to high schools and colleges. Purchasing a home close to a college is a great way to belong to a strong rental market.

6. Unexpected costs

Although the primary objective of buying an investment property is to generate revenue, you should be ready for abnormal expenses. As a result, you need to have a rough figure of the cost of replacing all main parts of the house; this should include the HVAC system, roof, and other elements. Set aside a reasonable amount of cash as a contingency measure. Always have this money available either in a savings account or via a credit card. You never know when an emergency might occur.

7. Property management

It is not easy to be a landlord, so you need to ask yourself whether you are willing to wake up as early as three a.m. to go and attend to an emergency at your property.

For most investors, they prefer to let a property management company handle everything. Most of these companies receive a 10% payment from the monthly rent.

Some landlords have no problem with the management fee because they find it reasonable; others decide to save the money and fix problems by themselves. This decision is yours to make, but it's one that you need to be careful about as the result could be critical.

Chapter 3: Running Your Rental Property

How to Add Value to Your Rental Property

As a rental property investor, you want to reduce costs so that you can make substantial money from your properties. However, limiting your spending to the point where your rentals aren't conducive for tenants to stay in isn't a good thing.

Typically, the objective of the rental investment is to add value. You want it to double in value from when you purchased it. There are different methods to employ that will add value, as well as expensive and advanced renovations that can be done:

1. Change the front appearance of the property

It is said that people create a perception of another person in seven seconds. This means that you don't need to spend much time developing a first impression. The same thing applies when you evaluate rentals. For that reason, making simple improvements, such as mowing the lawn, replacing the mailbox, painting the front door, and trimming long hedging bushes is important. By making these changes to your rental property, you increase the chances of getting a tenant to move in, and it adds top dollars to your income.

2. Confirm that the unit is well lit and smells nice for display

It is common sense to clean a unit before showing it. However, again, you need to make sure that the lights are on and blinds are open, to ensure that the unit is brightly lit when a potential tenant comes to view it. Remember: dark rooms are less welcoming.

Also spray air fresheners to make the rooms smell nice. A sense of smell is highly associated with memory; this means that if the property smells great, it will remain in the tenant's memory.

3. Don't just focus on showing, but also sell

If you think that you are just going to open the door and the prospect will be interested in your unit, then you are doing it wrong. There are three strategies that you can use to sell the showing of your unit:

- Build a rapport
- Apply anchors
- Employ reciprocation

If you are going to do the showings, you should at least use the first two. Establishing rapport means that you become friendly and interact with your prospects freely. Show a genuine interest in them. Ask them questions, and enjoy some moments with them. As you sell your property, make sure that you don't oversell. People always want to rent property from people they like.

When it comes to anchoring, people prefer a specific value for an unknown amount before they can approximate the quantity. That means that if you are going to tell your prospect that the house is 1,300 square feet, you would have anchored in their mind that the house is about 1,300 square feet. So, if you ask them to say what they feel the house is, they will perhaps mention the value in the range between 1,100 and 1,400. On the other hand, if you were to say that the house is about 900 square feet, then they will form an idea that the house is too small. In other words, their response will vary depending on what you anchor.

However, there are times when anchors can be qualitative. So you can decide to say things like, "I love this house" or "The kitchen in this house is beautiful" before you walk in with your prospect. Lastly, in some situations, especially in the hot markets, you can use the rule of reciprocation. According to this rule, people will always feel obliged to repay invitations, gifts, and favors. Psychologically, this will work when people want to rent from you if you do something good for them.

This can make you come out as manipulative, but don't expect to persuade someone to rent your property if you offer them five dollars. If you have a fantastic property, the rule of reciprocation will set yours aside from your competitors. This kind of discount in your advertising campaign may further generate traffic to your properties.

4. Don't start with a low price

The basic principle with apartment rents is that if the rate of occupancy is meager, you cannot increase the rent. However, with houses, it is different because it's difficult to tell what to rent a place for—although you can get some idea on RentRange, Zillow, and Craigslist.

Sound advice is to look at renting a house from the angle that you can repair a property that is priced high, but it is difficult to fix one that is priced too low. Why? If you under rent a property, then you will have to stick with that figure. However, when you set the price too high, then you'll easily tell that it is too expensive because no one wants to rent it. Then you can quickly make some changes by reducing the price. So, you should begin at the top if you think you can get prospects.

You don't want to mess this up. Every day that passes with a unit still on the market means that you are losing rent. And when there is a high vacancy, or it is in the winter season, and fewer people are searching for a rental, you need to become more aggressive. But in most cases, it is advised to begin with a higher range.

5. Add a dryer and washer

Appliances are a small investment, so it might not seem worth the money to buy a brand-new washer-dryer for your rental property. But getting one from Craigslist, or a different vendor may reduce the cost. The most important thing is that renters are interested in a specific level of convenience in the living space, and they are ready to pay some good money to get it. You can increase the rental price tag by $80 per month just by adding a washer to the dryer. If you apply the same approach, you may pay off your investment—even if it is new machinery—in just a year. And after this, you will be earning the extra money.

6. Change the exterior

So much attention is concentrated on the inside of the home, but without any outside appeal, prospective buyers may not want to rent or even walk in to look at the work you have done. You don't need to pay top dollar for repainting a home to make it attractive. Even something simple like power-washing the driveway, the exterior of the property, sidewalk, and other dingy-looking areas can change the mind of your prospects.

Consider redesigning the front door if you want a quick project to boost the outside appeal. If you have a sturdy door, make arrangements to repaint it and add some accents, such as a kick plate. If you replace the old door, it will improve the value of the property while it changes the outside appeal.

7. Replace Carpeted floor

Prospective tenants tend to dislike carpets, which can be a disadvantage for your rental. Also, this type of flooring makes it hard to remove stains and scents; in other words, you may need to employ a professional company to clean it for you.

To avoid this long-term financial strain, invest in universal flooring. It can be a lighter color that doesn't reveal scratches and nicks easily. It may cost thousands of dollars for high-quality options; however, there are cost-effective choices, too, like bamboo, that have the same appearance and durability.

Lease Options and Purchase Sales Basics

In the late 1970s and 1980s, sales of lease options became common financing instruments These were used as a means to overcome alienation clauses included in the mortgage. However, they have other advantages too. Proponents suggested that this was not a sale since it was not a lease, but the argument of courts has been different.

There are three different types of lease options and lease purchase agreements. The documents are similar but different in the more exceptional details. The difference is because of the state-specific aspect and the various laws in each state. It is wise to consult with a rental property investment attorney before you strike an agreement with a seller.

Option

In this case, the buyer is supposed to pay the seller option cash for permission to use the property later when he or she signs up for the option arrangement. This particular option can be substantial, or even as little as $1.

Both the seller and buyer agree to the buying price during this time, or the buyer can accept to pay the value of the market during the time the option is carried out. While this is negotiable, most buyers want to secure the future buying price at the start.

The timeline of the option agreement is discussed as well, but the most common is between one to three years.

Option money isn't refundable easily, and nobody wants to buy the property during the option time; though the buyer can sell the option to someone else.

The buyer isn't forced to purchase the property. That means if the buyer doesn't apply the option and buy the property towards the end of the option, the option will generally expire.

Lease option

A lease option tends to work in the same manner. The potential buyer will pay the seller cash for permission to buy the property later. A lease option provides the potential buyer more flexibility than a lease purchase, which requires the renter to buy the property at the end of the rental period.

The property owner may decide to charge the renter a premium for the option to buy the property, maybe in form of a higher rental payments. It can still be a one-time cash payment which resembles the premium paid for an option in the financial markets. This is not a deposit on the purchase of the property so it is non-refundable. The amount varies from a token $100 to 5% of the expected purchase price.

In the agreement, the property owner may choose to apply some of the higher rental fee toward the purchase price if the renter implements the option.

The length of the option can be any period on which the property owner and potential buyer agree, but it is usually 1-3 years. The lease option contract can also define the property's purchase price at the beginning of the lease.

Lease purchase

This is another variation on the same theme with some small changes. The buyer will pay the seller option cash for the permission to buy the property later. Then both the buyer and seller strike a deal on the buying price; usually, higher than that in the current market.

During the time of the option, a buyer can accept to lease the rental from the seller for a certain price. The terms of the lease-purchase can be negotiated, but the most common is one to two years.

The buyer seeks financing from the bank and pays the seller the whole amount when the term ends. Option money may fail to work toward the down payment, but a specific monthly amount of the lease payment is channeled to the purchase price. The monthly lease amount is mostly higher than the fair market rental value for the same reason.

Remember that option money is not refundable. As a result, it is impossible for anyone else to purchase the property unless the buyer defaults. Typically, it is hard for the buyer to decide on the purchase-lease option without approval from the seller.

Generally, buyers have the responsibility of maintaining the property and pay all expenses during the upkeep period. It may include taxes and insurance, and they are merely obliged to buy the property.

Using a lease to purchase property

A lease purchase refers to the agreement between the landlord and tenant that provides the tenant with the option to buy the property at a certain point in the future. The nature of this real estate transaction can change because all the terms of a lease purchase are open for negotiation. For example, it may or may not comprise the set price. But when it does, the cost can be the appreciated value of the property during the time of buying.

Lease purchase payments

In general, the seller will want the tenant to pay a non-refundable amount in advance to "purchase" the option to buy the property. It is usually referred to as the "option" payment and can be any figure. This "locks in" the tenant's option to buy, even when the landlord decides to change his or her mind.

Together with the purchase price, the term of a lease defines the size of the down payment and the schedule. The parties can then strike a deal regarding a portion of the rent getting paid towards the down payment. That would then mean an increase in rent each month. However, some buyers may consider it a means of forced savings towards a down payment.

Benefits of lease purchase for tenants

Different advantages come when a person decides to lease a property with the option to buy it later. Below are the reasons why an individual may decide to lease a home:

- They want some time to fix credit problems so that they can be allowed to seek a traditional mortgage.

- They want time to save up for a down payment and currently don't want to lose the home.

- They have invested significantly in the property through repairs and improvements. Typically, the value of this work can work towards a down payment and against the purchase price.

The advantages of the lease to sellers

The lease-purchase can benefit owners of a rental property too:

- The up-front payment plan can increase the investment return, and it is the owner who remains with it even if the tenant doesn't buy the home.

- The owner can get a reasonable price for the home early.

- By providing a lease-purchase option, it can attract tenants that are interested in long-term occupancy.

- When a tenant plans to own a home, he or she can be willing to keep it in good condition for the whole period of the lease.

The bottom line is that if you own a property that isn't selling and you must relocate, or you're a real estate investor with different properties, purchasing a lease may be the best option to lock down a sale and great price for your property. If you don't have a home or experience credit problems, a lease purchase can work for you too as a tenant.

Regardless of the side of the lease-purchase agreement, it can be a win-win for both. However, because all the features of the private deal are up for individual parties, you need to pay attention to your interests and needs when you hammer out the terms.

Marketing Tips for Advertising Your Rental Property Quickly

A vacant rental property generates losses, especially when you have a mortgage and no tenants have moved in; in a few months, this can result in a significant financial loss. To reduce the time that your property remains vacant, you need to have an effective marketing plan. Your goal is to attract good and long-term tenants. In a market with many vacancies and stiff competition, it is vital for your property to stand out in the best way possible. Promoting your real estate business is an essential task, and there is no time that you can afford to lose. Rental property investment is a "people business". This means that you must be ready to communicate, connect, and build a relationship with people. The majority of these interactions depend on the way you decide to market your properties.

Maybe you have been following every bit of advice and the steps given by experienced investors on how to attract tenants, but for some reason, none of your efforts have succeeded. If you are disappointed with your rental, here are a few tips that you can apply to get your rental investment property off the market and begin generating good returns:

Quality photos

It is said that a picture is worth a thousand words. In the case of rental property investment, a photo can be said to be worth a few thousand bucks. In this modern age, you must create attention-grabbing photographs of your real estate property to grab the interest of prospects. Whether you want to upload the photographs online or in a publication, you need to ensure that your photos are quality and professional.

When you have quality photos of your rental property, it will encourage people to stay a bit longer at your property. Even if you don't seek the services of a photographer, there are some great ways to polish your property photos. Consider the following:

> • **The outside shot is the most important.** The first photo is always the exterior side of your property. This photo is famous because it can either attract attention or chase away prospects. Keep in mind that the first impression is crucial. For this photo to look elegant, you need to take it after sunset, half an hour before the sun goes down, or early in the morning. Twilights shots can emerge with the exterior lights on. An excellent exterior photo should be the hook that captures the sight of prospective clients.

> • **Keep the photos straight.** Look for a tripod. By using a wide-angle lens resting on a tripod, a great SLR camera will make your photograph straight. Don't use smartphone cameras because they are not wide enough to take smaller spaces, and it will make your area appear cramped. In most occasions, you will require a wide-angle lens about 28mm. A travel tripod will make sure that you take straight photographs. Only a few people will spend the time looking at a property photo that appears to be sinking into the earth. If you can't get a tripod, make sure that you find a bubble level and use that to maintain the shape of your photos.

- **Remove the flash.** Don't use the flash; instead, allow natural light to shine and maintain the surrounding of the space. Taking photos using the flash may overexpose the property, and this tends to make your property unattractive and misconstrue depth. Besides, the flash can reveal visual flaws.

- **Decide on the photos you want to show:** Studies have found that online rental hunters spend around 60% of their time on a listing just looking at the photographs. And that is why you can't afford to use dull photos for advertising your property. In case you hire a photographer to take your photos, make sure that you know the kind of photographs that you don't want to use, and how best to use the photographs to grab the attention of renters. It is vital that your photos pass on the message that you care about the presentation and the property. Remember that photos don't just speak about your property; they also show that you care. The reputation that it builds should be that of a person who is professional and caring.

Comprehensive listing

If there is something that you must avoid, it is making your prospective tenants struggle to identify the details of your property. Most people hunting for rentals nowadays turn to online platforms and want to make quick comparisons. If you are not clear on things such as amenities and pet policies, it will chase people away. People want to know a lot about the property before they move in or even commit to tracking it. It is advised that you be as specific as possible and avoid using flowery language—that doesn't work well on online rental platforms. Instead, focus on your message of quality and excellent service. If you want to offer a quality property and pleasant service, then tell them. But avoid all the flowery language that describes the beauty and calmness of the place. Tenants are interested in knowing what they are going to receive and want many different options to select from.

Internet savvy advertising

In this day and age, it will be difficult for you to grab the attention of people if you don't stay updated with the changes in the internet and advertising sector. If you plan to advertise your property on a website, make sure that the ads are well timed. Studies indicate that listings set on Fridays receive more views, and homes are sold faster than those placed on other days. The same can apply for rentals. Don't be afraid to put up your listing more than once.

There are many methods for your online property marketing besides just posting a listing. You can, for example, record and put up a video tour of your rental property on YouTube, allowing other potential tenants to see and become interested in your property from the comfort of their homes.

By taking the time to promote your property, you will affect the overall investment. It can change the whole impression, leading to more tenants and a profitable venture.

Learn more about your demographic

When you are targeting a particular type of family or individual to rent your property, it is necessary to consider that in all your advertising strategies. If you are going to target families with children, for example, build amenities on your property that will attract children and highlight them when writing a description of your rental. The same level of consideration should be applied to every audience. If you're targeting seniors, then you need to identify things that seniors like in a property and let those aspects feature in your description. Promote your property at local recreation places and workout centers (where families may likely see it), and post advertisements in local grocery stores and daycare centers around your property.

Find elegant signage

Look for a real "For Rent" sign. While there are some signs that you can get from the hardware store, most of these are common and not unique. Just remember that the real estate market is competitive, and you need to be different from the rest, and this includes your signage. You can make an order for custom, cheap signs on the internet from places such as buildasign.com. Add a few quick, important details such as monthly rent, number of bedrooms, and whether or not the utilities are available. Don't forget to include a contact number and email address. When you set up a sign for the world to see, make sure that it is close to the street. If you want to go all out, then you can spend some more dollars and place a few signs in the yard.

Open house

An open house can be another strategy to gain exposure for your property. Open houses don't cause the same stress on viewers as the official show. Usually, they will grab the attention of curious people. Allow passersby to look inside your property by opening blinds and permitting users to take a glance. Also, if you have multiple properties to rent, you can create flyers for tenants to see everything that you have. Regardless of the property that they rent, the purpose of an open house is to bring attention to your property.

Use the power of networking

Take advantage of social media sites to spread the word. Facebook and Twitter are great platforms to reach out to your friends that may not be aware of your property.

Think about how you can advertise in the neighborhood, like creating and sending postcards marketing your property in the neighborhood. The people who live close may likely know someone who is hunting for a house to rent. If you sweeten the deal a little, using something like a gift card, the chances are that you won't wait long before people move in.

Marketing a rental property requires that you plan well, be ready to try new things, and never think that you are above trying some things. Sometimes, you need to get out of your comfort zone to make things happen.

Secrets to Maintaining Profitability in Rental Property

1. Set a budget for and monitor expenses

It may surprise you that you need to spend some money to maintain your rental portfolio. That aside, some landlords don't estimate what their expenses may be for the current year. If you are one of them, or if you don't plan for your expenses, then each cost that does occur will shock you.

By creating a budget, though, you can estimate the amount of money that you will spend, and how much you will receive. Also, if you are planning to include investors in your business, it is essential to have great financial projection.

It is not difficult to create a budget. If you have had the property for more than a year, all you need to do is revisit your payment records. If you have accounting software, this is as simple as clicking for a report. If that is not the case, scan through your previous year and arrange everything into a spreadsheet. Let's assume that if no huge expenses have emerged, you can estimate that what you will pay in expenses will be the same as the previous year.

2. Set aside some capital

Improvements in capital can help add value to your rental. According to accounting, capital improvements aren't a one-year expense like utility expense. These have been capitalized into the value of the building.

Examples include replacement of the roof and new furnaces. You can also include significant renovations, windows, new appliances, and windows if they add to the value of the property. If you don't set aside some bucks to cover these things, when they emerge, you may end up reaching your budget when the furnace requires some replacement.

3. Organize for preventative maintenance

Some landlords wait for a problem to happen before they send a person to conduct a repair. This can be costly, as the tenant may not notify you of a problem until it worsens. Small things can turn into big things, and it is hard to wait for a tenant to decide when you should perform some maintenance on your investment.

Proactive repairs are vital because they help fix a problem before it escalates and becomes a major expense. The leaking tap in the bathroom might become large if the tenant doesn't bother to tell you. The smoke detector with a dead battery is not secure for the tenant and becomes a liability. The broken gutter, if not repaired early, will result in a water leak in your roof. And the list goes on and on. You can choose to address these small things in a reasonable time versus fixing them when they get out of hand.

Reducing expenses is a method that the landlord can use to limit the overhead placed on the building, mainly by reducing utility expenses on a multi-family apartment.

How to Create a Property Investment Business Model

Almost everyone who does well in music, business, career, sports, and other areas in life started with a solid plan. Even if that plan is something like, "I think I can buy this device for $100 and sell it for $130," that is still a statement of what the business can do and how it will generate profit.

However, most, especially the wannabe property investors, begin without a basic plan. Usually, people have nothing more than a vague idea—"Property prices rise, so it's a great investment" or "Many wealthy people tend to own property."

You may think that spending all day planning is wasting time, compared to getting out and searching for properties and thus beginning to make money, but professional real estate investors will tell you that every business that lives up to its goal has a solid plan.

Or, to put it more plainly, almost everyone who doesn't start with a plan becomes frustrated with where they end up. No matter how much money, effort, and time you pump into your business, without a plan, you can't reach far.

So, what does a property investment business model look like?

It doesn't need to be 100 pages of projections and beautiful charts. Successful investors have the most straightforward plan that can fit on the back of an index card. That means that you can memorize it quickly and use it to implement every decision that you make.

But before you get that simple plan, you may need to involve your brain in some severe brainstorming and thinking.

It doesn't look easy, but at least it is simple. Your plan needs to address:

- Your current state at the moment.

- Where you want to reach (your target goal).

- The actions you are going to implement to reduce the gap.

Your Current State at the Moment

It is impossible to plan a journey if you don't know where you are going to start.

Finding out your starting point is the simplest thing to do because it includes information that you already know or easily know. You need to be clear about:

- The amount of money that you need to invest.

- The amount of savings that you need to assign to property investment in the coming years.

- The amount of time that you can invest every week or month.

- The knowledge and skills that you can apply to your property business.

Being aware of the amount of money that you can invest should be easy, but it is vital to speak to a mortgage broker to confirm that you have borrowing options. This is important because it will define your total investment amount. A broker can also tell you about the options you have for releasing equity from your own home—if that is something you would like to consider.

It is also good to consider the "emergency fund" that you want to have in cash and deduct from your investable funds. It is advised to have at least six months' expenses in the bank at any given time; the worst thing is to pump all your money into investments.

Where You Want to Reach

So far, you know where you are going to start from, but where do you want to reach? This is another way of asking you to define your goal.

Of course, you want to be "rich" or "build a future"; however, what does that mean for you?

And most importantly again, when do you want to achieve this?

You may be shocked to learn how much effort and energy is involved in responding to these questions correctly. It is easy to say things like, "Enough to fund my lifestyle" and assume that it might be an income of $10,000 per month, but it is a different thing to lock honestly at the ideal lifestyle and decide what a reasonable figure is.

The same thing applies for "when", and it is something that is often ignored; however, it highlights the foundation of investment decisions.

For instance, consider two property options:

1. Property A will generate a return investment of 15% but will never increase in value.

2. Property B will generate a return of 7% but will increase in value in the next decade.

If you plan to build a monthly income within three years, then property A is likely going to be the best choice. However, you are unlikely to experience growth in the next few years, and you may currently need to optimize for cash in the bank.

Alternatively, if you have made a choice that you want to achieve your goal probably in the next decade, then Property B is the best to go with. It is a gamble, but you will have enough time for it to occur, and when it does happen, your returns will surpass the higher rental income you could have made from property A.

This is just an example to show you why making even simple decisions in your business property can be difficult if you don't have a basic plan: where you want to end up and when you want it to happen.

So, at this point in the plan, you should:

- Evaluate your finances to create an honest picture of your current status.

- Take the time to think about where you want to reach and when.

It is a great start, but for most people, it will not produce the best insight, and the gap between where they are and where they want to be will appear impossibly large.

Chapter 4: Analyzing a Rental Property

Rental properties are the most popular type of real estate properties across the world. This is because they are easy to control, and most new investors consider it the starting ground of their careers.

However, if you plan to invest in a rental property, how are you going to make sure that it is the right property to invest in? How can you tell that the property will return a profit that is enough to handle all its expenses?

To answer these questions, rental property analysis comes into play. It is the process of analyzing an investment property to measure its viability and the amount of profit that it can achieve as an income property.

When conducting a rental property analysis, there are several factors to consider. Some affect the performance of the property directly, while others are used to calculate its returns.

Below are the most critical factors used to analyze a rental property:

Location

In real estate investing, location is crucial as it can profoundly affect a property's performance, define the marketing strategy, and the kinds of tenants that you want to attract to the investment. For example, if you invest in a rental property that is close to a college, you will be targeting students or members of the institutions to make the best out of the location.

Rental Strategy

Picking the correct rental approach for your income property can either make or break your career. Before you begin to rent out your property, it is vital that you look at the different options available. There are two primary rental strategies to apply, and both cannot operate on the same property:

- Long-term properties

- Short-term properties

For you to select between the two, you need to use a rental property analysis tool to help you learn the most profitable method.

The Type of Property

Each category of real estate property has its advantages and disadvantages. When carrying out a comparative analysis, the type of property that you invest in is essential. A comparative market analysis doesn't have to consider all the securities in an area; however, it should only involve securities that are similar to your property. This should include the type of property, age, size, and other factors.

Target Tenants

A tenant is a person that resides in your income property and either pays a weekly or monthly rent in exchange for his or her stay. Maybe the most exciting aspect of rental properties is that the tenants renting your property are the ones responsible for paying your mortgage and other expenses.

There are different categories of tenants, and you are required to customize your marketing techniques and home design to match the kind of tenants that you want to attract.

Rental Income and Cash Flow

Rental income of a property refers to the amount of rent that a person receives from tenants on a daily, weekly, or monthly basis. On the other hand, cash flow refers to the amount of initial loss or profit that the property generates.

The cash flow of a rental income property describes the primary indicator of profitability. Cash flow is either negative or positive; it depends on the amount of money that you lose or make. If you want to determine the cash flow, you merely need to pick the rental income value and exclude all the costs and expenses associated with the property from the same value.

Vacancy and Occupancy Rates

The rate of vacancy refers to the time that a property remains vacant, and the rate of occupancy refers to when it is occupied.

In a typical case, the rate of occupancy of a property has to be 100% and will grant you the chance to make a profit from the rental property for the whole year.

The rate of vacancy is determined as an expense. After computing the profits that you earn from rental income and subtracting all the costs, you can proceed to multiply the amount by the rate of occupancy to find the cash flow of the property.

Cap Rate

This is a metric involved in determining the return on investment of a rental income depending on the current market value.

The formula for finding the cap rate includes:

Cap Rate = (Net Operating Income)/ Current Market Value) x 100

This metric indicates the profitability of the property. The value of the cap rate is also displayed as a percentage. It represents the amount of profit that you want to make every year compared to the original price of the property. The metric does not include the method used to finance, and it will assume that the property was entirely bought with cash.

Cash on Cash Return

Even though the money on cash return is applied in determining the return on investment of an income property, it is different from the cap rate metric because it factors in the method of financing. Even more accurate is that the cash on cash return only includes the actual funds invested in the property's purchase.

Therefore, if you buy a property with 80% borrowed money and 20% cash, the cash on the return metric will only apply 20% cash to its computation.

The formula used to determine the cash on cash return includes:

Cash on Cash Return = (NOI/Cash invested) x 100

The cash on cash return value is also expressed as a percentage and reveals the amount of money that one can make in a year out of the total amount of cash that is invested in the property.

Comparative Market Analysis

For you to make an accurate evaluation of a rental property, you will have to make a comparison with similar securities in the area. A comparative market analysis is useful to help you compare single or several securities with other properties in the market to know whether the properties are doing well.

By using comparative market analysis, you can assess where the highest ability is in the market by making a comparison of the various metrics and values.

For instance, if you make a comparative analysis, and the outcome reveals that the average cap rate of the market is 4%, then the properties with a cap rate of 7% do well above the market average.

It is that easy.

When it comes to investing in rental property, understanding how to run the numbers is necessary for your success in generating profit, and making the right investment.

As seen previously, there are many things to factor in when analyzing possible rental properties. Whether you like it or not, when you get started in real estate investment, you will be taking your financial future into your own hands.

And this can be worrying to most people.

However, it can also be compelling to many people. Usually, when people start to invest in rental property, they always feel afraid of making a mistake or purchasing a "bad property".

But the truth is that many helpful materials can guide you.

And when it comes to analyzing prospective deals, there is no room for subjectivity.

You don't need to be a genius to see the future or memorize numbers; you only need to be aware of the numbers and a tool that assists you in computing the return. For that reason, if you are curious about the fact that anyone can invest in rental property, even if you don't know where to start, don't worry. This book will help you!

What numbers are you supposed to be familiar with when running a property analysis?

In general, an analysis of a property involves a set of numbers that are connected to the property and computing them determines the type of return the property will generate.

If you don't know all of these numbers or they are not accurate, it will result in an inaccurate approximation of the ROI or the estimated monthly cash flow.

The truth is that, in some cases, it may take a little while to identify these numbers. It may require a phone call to a real estate agent to generate an estimate of some important numbers.

But the phone calls are critical to ensuring that you have accurate estimates of the return.

Let's look at some of the numbers that you need to have to help you analyze:

1. Taxes

Find out your total tax for the property for the whole year.

2. List price

This is the price that the seller is asking for the property.

3. Utilities

If you're going to pay for services or utilities on the property, you may need to ask your sellers for information on the type of utilities that have cost them in the past.

4. Capital expenditure

This is similar to building for a reserve fund. The capital expenditure is linked with large items that you will have to replace that are expensive. It is possible to account for saving a specific percentage each month to channel it toward the capital expenditure.

5. Vacancy rate

One thing that is true about rental property is that it will be vacant from time to time. This will cost you money and affect your ROI. However, you can account for this at the start by running an analysis of your local area. Real estate agents may provide an estimated percentage of the vacancy rate in your local area.

6. Down payment

How much are you going to put down on the rental property? The possible loan product that you want to use may show what a down payment amount is going to be.

7. Mortgage term

The loan product will determine the conditions. In general, you'll see the terms in increments of fifteen, twenty, or even 30 years. Typically, on a conventional loan, you're going to focus on a 20% down payment on a 30-year term.

If you enter these numbers into a property analyzer, it will automatically compute the ROI and forecast a monthly cash flow so that you can get the right estimate on whether the property fulfills your investing goals.

Tips for Running Numbers on Property

When it comes to analyzing numbers on properties, this is the section that you want to be accurate. You don't want to miss anything. Remember, when you invest in rental property, the numbers have to determine the most significant *investment* decision for you—so leave emotion out of the equation. Besides that, you need tools to help you remain on track:

1. Look for a property analyzer

When you are starting, you may ask yourself how you can find the numbers highlighted earlier and what to do with them.

Most people aren't going to sit down and build a comprehensive spreadsheet that runs the numbers with no sweat; however, the internet has useful resources that can help you calculate numbers on properties. You can look for free analyzers and apps that are designed to estimate your mortgage and provide you with an idea of what your mortgage may look like so that you don't struggle to identify this on your own.

The greatest thing about most of these property analyzers is that you will need to enter all the information about the property, and it will automatically compute your ROI and cash flow.

This will allow you to make your choice pretty quickly regarding whether the property fulfills your return on investment goals. If it does, then you can begin to narrow down the path of looking for more information and scheduling a demo.

On the other hand, if it fails to meet your ROI goals, then it is going to be easy to say no and continue looking.

Not only does owning a tool make it easy to qualify or disqualify a property for you, but it can generally save you a lot of time.

2. Numbers are black and white

For some people, this creates a feeling of relief. But for those who prefer a gray section, this can prove difficult. However, the truth is that numbers aren't subjective. There are data and information that you will come across on every property that will let you run a black and white analysis of it.

In the field of rental property investing, there is some subjectivity in the decisions that you make. These include the kind of tenant that you allow in your property, location, and the condition of the property.

These things don't look black and white, but when you turn to numbers, it has to be.

When you do an analysis of the property, and it shows your predicted ROI and cash flow, then it is high time you trust it.

Ignore the emotion and concentrate on what the property is going to deliver to you and whether that is going to help you realize the goals you have set as an investor.

Steps to Follow to Determine the Value of Your Property Accurately

Step 1: Determine your annual gross rental yield

Multiply your monthly market rent by twelve, and you will get the annual rent. Next, select the yearly rent and perform a division of the price with the latest property market price. For instance:

$3,000/month = $36,000/year, $36,000/$500,000 = 7.2% gross rental yield

Step 2: Make a comparison of gross rental yield to the risk-free rate

Risk-free refers to ten-year bond production. All investments should feature a risk-free premium rate. If the annual gross rental yield is lower than the risk-free rate, then you should try to bargain.

Step 3: Compute the annual net rental yield

This yield represents your net operating income. It can be computed by getting your gross yearly rent and subtracting the mortgage interest, maintenance costs, and property taxes. The net rental outcome can be different for every investor since certain places have much more money than others.

Step 4: Now compare the rental yield to the risk-free rate

Typically, the yield of the net rental should either be higher or equal to the risk-free rate. You'll pay the principal down over time and then increase the return of the rented apartment. If everything runs well, rents will rise, and your property will go up in price.

Step 5: Now determine the price-earnings ratio of your property

This is the market value for your property divided by the net running profit at that time.

Step 6: Predict the future property price and rental expectations

The real deal is to forecast expectations correctly. As a rental property investor, you want to make use of abnormal events. The best method to use to predict the future is to compare what happened in the previous years through online charts and create realistic expectations about the local employment growth. Is the city continuing to expand in terms of development, or are there restrictions placed? Are employers moving out of the town or joining it?

Step 7: Run different scenarios

The first thing is to establish the price of your property and rental forecasts and then run different scenarios.

Step 8: Be aware of taxes and depreciation

Nearly all expenses associated with owning a rental property are taxable. Another exciting thing that you need to know is depreciation.

Step 9: Look for comparable sales

The easiest way that you can look for comparable sales of the last six to twelve months is to use an online website like Zillow.com. Here you're going to see the sale history, tax records, and much more. You need to make a comparison of your target property asking price with the other sales. Then you can identify what has changed to ensure that you get the best deal.

Mistakes to Avoid While Analyzing Rentals

1. Don't underestimate or overestimate expenses

Once you begin analyzing your rental investment property, you will start to realize that you cannot always find accurate numbers on a deal.

When this situation happens, you need to apply your experience and estimate—but one thing that you should not do is overestimate.

It is slightly better for the numbers to drop on the last day that they appear. If you have a habit of overestimating numbers, this has the possibility of turning a good deal bad fast. If the numbers are very close to begin with and you even overestimate by $200 on something, that can cause what looked like a profitable business to be a bust.

2. Don't trust every word from the mouth of a seller

When you ask for numbers for prospective deals, then you should always follow it up with another request for documents to verify what the seller says. You have the right to request for verification of numbers when you feel that something isn't right. Asking for confirmation is another way to protect your money.

The truth is that there are different things that you must consider when you are about to start investing in rental property. However, one of the most critical areas that you need to dedicate your time well to is in analyzing deals.

It is important to remember that while analyzing an area of investment, it is possible to make mistakes. Some of these mistakes can cost you a lot. This is not meant to scare you, but it's just another way to reinforce the need to use the correct numbers when you analyze and to make sure that you don't end up using wrong numbers you receive from realtors and sellers.

The thought of mastering the techniques of analyzing investment properties may seem overwhelming, but with daily practice and then using the right tools, you will become a pro at finding a property, investigating, and purchasing a rental property.

Chapter 5: Finance Your Rental Property

Investing in rental property is a great move, but which methods can you use to finance a rental property?

In general, financing is the most challenging part of purchasing rental income properties. Most people spend the majority of their time on this stage. However, if you don't need to do so, especially when you understand all the available options that you can use to finance your rental property and become familiar with what to consider to pick the best option, you'll finally agree that it is not hard to finance a rental property. So, you need to be familiar with the different options of financing a rental property and when it's right to use each of them. To assist you in learning and selecting a financing method, here is how you can finance your rental property:

1. Cash

This is one of the easiest ways of financing a rental property if you already have the money because the loan amount is zero. However, there are also drawbacks. For instance, you'll be missing out on the pros of leveraging. Leveraging is using money from other people to finance your rental property. If you don't leverage, then your return on investment, including cash on cash return, will start to decline.

All cash is the best method to finance a rental property when you know that you have a high income, you plan to make small purchases every year, or you want to put your money somewhere without bothering about the returns.

What is the best cash on cash return?

You will rarely hear someone talk about cash on cash return beyond the field of rental property investment. Most investments are determined by what is called the return on investment but not with the cash on cash return. For one to compute the ROI, it is a must to know the amount of cash generated from an investment. But it is not easy to estimate the amount of money that a rental can generate.

As a result, it doesn't sound reasonable to bring in the idea of ROI when deciding between whether to buy or not buy an investment property. So, the most popular and straightforward unit applied is the cash on cash return. That is calculated by conducting a division of the cash flow using the amount of cash initially invested.

When it comes to good cash on cash return, experts have their numbers. Some suggest that any number above 8% is okay while others disagree. Experts that disagree advise cash on a return of 20% or more. The cash on cash return is not fixed but changes from one location to another.

Since cash on cash return is a modest metric, it doesn't promise to say everything about a rental property. For instance, it doesn't consider appreciation in real estate. Therefore, it is just a signal on whether a real estate investment can be a great idea or not. But before you make your final decision, it is essential to conduct an in-depth analysis that will provide you with the return you are looking for:

1. Purchase as an owner-occupant

When you purchase a rental home as an owner-occupant, you'll be able to receive the best financing deals. You can secure a homeowner-grade mortgage that is guaranteed for 30 years with a minimum down payment of 3.5%. The bank will generally pay your taxes as well as the insurance from an escrow account, which you then pay every month as part of the deal. You can again purchase another property as an owner-occupant and repeat the same process once more.

That said, it is necessary to be careful that you don't overuse this process because it will appear in your credit, and because you can only get some of these loans, you may hit a snag and need to turn elsewhere for other options.

It is the right way to finance a rental property if you are new to the rental business, or you want to hold a few rentals as a side job.

2. Small community finance by bank

This is slightly different from the traditional bank loan. Unlike big banks that have their operations in all states, small banks will work in small communities The big banks respect the guidelines, but small banks tend to maintain the loans in-house instead of selling them off to investors. They'll want to learn more about you. So, you need to be ready for a face-time visit and be prepared to network. Once it's approved, they will be pretty easy to work with.

Small banks also enjoy when your deals fall within their sphere. One of the best things about small banks is that they know much about equity partnerships because they strike deals in other areas of business, not only in the rental property. Therefore, if you're thinking about adding investors to purchase big properties with you, small banks can be helpful to ensure that you structure the loans for this kind of deal.

A small community finance bank is one of the best methods to finance a rental property if you want to involve yourself full time in real estate investment. Again, if you know that you're good at building relationships and networking, this could be the best approach.

3. Conventional bank loan

You may have heard about a traditional bank loan; it adheres to the principles set by Freddie Mac, which hasn't been supported by the federal government. With the presence of an investment property, the down payment can rise to 30%. However, the good thing about this is that the bank may have an approximate rental income from the property to support your ratio of debt to income. So, you should take the time to discuss this with your lender.

That said, your credit history, income, and credit score are significant for a traditional bank loan. This determines your ability to get approved and the rate of interest for the mortgage. You must be able to afford the mortgage, and the future income from the property should not be included in the equation.

This is the best method to finance a rental property when you know that you have a good credit history and an excellent income.

4. Private lender

Whether it's a family friend or just a private investor, sometimes using a private lender instead of a bank has advantages. For instance, you can negotiate the deal without any fear or worry because there are no requirements that have been set already. The loan qualification procedure takes a short time and is very complex. So, you're going to spend little money on costs related to the loan.

However, the rate of interest is often higher, and loans from private lenders are usually short term. So, you may want to look for a private lender where you can walk into a bank and make the private lender be refinanced out. But before you can do this, be sure that you can negotiate a fair deal with the private lender. Additionally, interact with different lenders before you decide whom to close the deal with.

This method is best to use when you know that you aren't "bankable". You should also be a good negotiator and confident that the rental property is going to generate profit.

5. Government mortgage programs

Did you know that it is possible to sign up for programs on how to finance a rental property? Government mortgage programs like USDA, FHA, and VA can assist prospective investors in purchasing rental properties for low down payments. For instance, FHA loans may come with a down payment of about 3.5%. Various types of programs may also lead to a small down payment.

6. Owner financing mortgages

You don't necessarily require a mortgage from government programs or banks to finance a rental property. You can borrow it from the sellers themselves. As funny as it may appear, it is possible to get a mortgage from rental property investors who plan to sell their properties. Everything regarding the loan is open for negotiation, which is a bonus. The problem is that many owners don't like this type of financing.

7. Hard money loans

Most of the strategies discussed aren't that risky or complicated; however, hard money loans are different. While these loans cover a large purchase sum, sometimes without a down payment, they are very risky for rental income properties. Part of their risk is because of the high interest rates and fees. Again, they are hard to find. So, if you are looking for a loan to pay for, and you are sure that you will pay it back on time, these loans may work well for you.

8. Fix-and-flip loans

The fix-and-flip loan is a type of hard money loan. This type of loan is used to finance a rental property investor who wants to do some maintenance or renovation. Like any other hard money loans, fix-and-flip loans have higher interest rates. For example, the rates on the following loans can go higher than 15%. Like all hard money loans, fix-and-flip loans vary depending on the value of the property instead of the credit of the investor.

There are different ways to finance a rental property, as shown from the above options. No method is right or wrong; it all depends on your time, why you are investing, and resources. We've looked at different options in this section, but you need to take the time and dive deeper into each method before you adopt it.

This should give you the drive and an idea on how to identify the best option to finance a rental property that matches your needs. In the next section are some creative ways to finance a rental property purchase.

Some more creative ways to finance a rental property

1. Seller financing

In this approach, you get a loan from the person who is selling you the property. Sometimes, when the seller wants to lend you money, it will be easier compared to going to the bank.

These deals work in some scenarios. The seller can decide to finance the down payment or the complete purchase. The seller may be another property investor or even the owner of the property.

The way to success with this is to make sure that you strike a reasonable agreement on the interest rate of the loan. If you don't have enough expertise in this area, it could be smart to work with an attorney. Regardless of how experienced you are, make sure that you agree to the terms of the loan in writing.

2. Partnerships

In this option, you form a partnership with another person. Then you can agree on a down payment. This is an excellent strategy if you have a family member who is interested in being part of the property investment, but maybe he or she is not involved in the daily work of collecting rent and performing the other duties of a landlord.

In this case, what happens is that one partner will contribute the money, and the other one will concentrate on the duties of being a landlord.

The key to success is to agree on how to share the income. It is advised to think of it as balancing the risk and reward with costs and benefits. Your partner takes the financial risk, but you dedicate all your energy to generate revenue through rent.

3. Retirement accounts

Most people who have worked for themselves have saved their retirement cash in an IRA. If you have a self-directed IRA, you will be granted permission to invest in a nontraditional asset. In other words, you can use the money in the self-directed IRA to run a rental property.

If you use this route, make sure that you have a word with your accountant first. Even with the presence of a software program that simplifies everything, rental property investment comes down to more of a hands-on investment than anything else in the stock market. Before you decide to get started, ensure that you make up your mind to invest the time and energy required to experience a return on investment.

Keep in mind that no matter how you decide to finance your rental property, ensure that you have enough paperwork ready to facilitate your success and regular income from the property you purchase. In other words, you need to invest in:

- Formal agreements with a professional seller who is willing to lend you money to buy a property.

- Legal documents such as LLC to define who does what and who gets what in compensation.

- Project the expected return from different investment types from a financial planner so that you can make various comparisons.

Chapter 6: Tips for Negotiation

What are some smart real estate negotiation tips? And as a rental investor, what is the best way to negotiate a real estate deal?

There is a specific objective when it comes to negotiating a deal to purchase an investment property. But what are the first things to do when you want to settle? Let's learn about the art of negotiation so that you can get the best price regardless of whether you are selling or buying.

To start, if you're planning to buy a property, take the time to understand exactly what you want from the investment. Are you looking forward to making money through the rise in property value over time, or do you want to earn cash flow and then purchase the property? Those are the two primary questions to consider.

Typically, you want both the property value to appreciate and also earn rental income. However, these two factors depend on the price you pay for the property and the way you pay. If you are going to do it through a loan, then the amount of interest you pay is going to be a critical factor in your cash flow.

The secret about negotiation is to avoid talking in numbers right away; instead, discuss what you are targeting and how both you and the agent can help each other. Negotiation is an art because it requires an agile mind, a calm demeanor, and firm reasoning. Of course, the ability to know when a deal is worth pursuing and when to walk away or buy the property is crucial.

In rental investment properties, you can negotiate on anything, whether it is the payment conditions, the price, the rental income, and the furniture for the rental property. Everything in real estate can be negotiated. Negotiations are especially important when you purchase an investment property because it is the best way to strike a deal for yourself as a rental property investor. Although new rental property investors may not know the most critical negotiation skills for a rental investment, those who are experienced, particularly those who are successful, are likely to be experts in negotiating the best deal. This chapter aims to teach you the tips to use while settling a deal to assist you in mastering the art of bargaining in rental investment properties.

New Guidelines

First, negotiation starts with the general rule that people like to be understood and accepted. For a long time, listening has been the cheapest but most effective tool that one can use. By listening carefully, you show empathy and an honest effort to understand the other person.

Become a Mirror

If there is something that separates good negotiators from bad negotiators, it is that good ones are always ready for surprises.

Good negotiators will challenge the assumptions that many people choose to accept either on faith or in arrogance. For that reason, they are emotionally open to all probabilities and intellectually flexible to situations.

Negotiations are not a battle of arguments. People who consider negotiations as a battle of cases often get disturbed by voices in their head. Negotiation is a journey of discovery. Your role is to discover as much information as you can.

To silence the many voices in your mind, make an effort to concentrate on what the other person wants to say. Your role is to try and understand what they want and make them feel secure enough to say so.

It is important to remember that negotiations cannot take place if listening is not granted. Listening, in this case, means giving the other person the time to speak, validate their emotions, and build enough trust and safety for a conversation to start.

Don't be quick to rush. One of the most common mistakes that negotiators make is that they always push the negotiations too fast. If you rush, people will begin to feel like they are not being heard, and you risk damaging the rapport and trust that you have built.

When it comes to negotiators, three kinds of voices are involved:

> **1. The late-night FM DJ voice**: For this one, apply it selectively to pass across your message. Just keep your voice low, calm, and slow. After you are done, you can then build a mandate of authority and trustworthiness without causing some defensiveness.

> **2. Playful voice:** This should be your default voice and that of a good-natured individual. The secret here is to relax and keep a smile while you talk.

> **3. Assertive or direct voice:** This particular voice is rarely used, but when applied, it may cause problems and create pushback.

Always wear a smile on your face. When people experience a positive state of mind, they think fast and are likely to work together and solve a problem. Positivity builds mental agility in both you and the other party.

You can decide to be direct and straight to the point by creating a safety tone of voice that says, "I'm doing fine, you're doing well; thus, we can figure things out."

Look at the assumptions and apply negotiation to evaluate it rigorously.

Mirrors create magic. Try and repeat the last three words of what the other person has just said. Many people are scared of different things and attracted to what is similar. Mirroring is a technique of emulating similarity. It is essential because it serves as a bonding mechanism. When should you mirror the other person? If you want to encourage the other person to bond with you, buy your side time to reorganize, keep the conversation going, and support your counterparts to disclose their strategy.

By repeating what people say, the other party will possibly explain what was just said and maintain the connection.

Avoid Feeling Their Pain; Instead, Label It

Technical empathy is the process of understanding the feelings and mindset of your counterpart and listening to what is driving those feelings so that you can ascertain your influence in all directions. This may involve drawing attention to both emotional challenges and potential avenues to reach an agreement.

If you can carefully look at another person's face, gestures, and tone of voice, your brain will start to match with theirs in a process called "neural resonance", and that makes us understand what they think and feel.

If you want to enhance your skills in neural resonance, then you should practice. Just turn your attention to a person who is talking close to you, or even look at a person being interviewed on the TV. While they speak, begin to imagine that you are that person. Visualize yourself in the position they are explaining and add as much detail as possible.

Labeling is a method used to validate the emotion of another person by showing approval. Name the feeling someone expresses and demonstrate how you identify with the person's experiences. This will bring you close to a person even without asking external aspects that you have no clue about.

The first thing to labeling is to identify the other person's state of emotions.

The secret to detecting feelings is to be mindful of changes that people experience when they respond to external events. In most cases, these events reflect your words. Once you see an emotion, the next thing is to label it aloud. Labels can be in the form of questions or statements; the only difference lies in the way you choose to end the sentence. Regardless of the way you end it, labels will always start with almost the same words:

- "It sounds like…"

- "It appears like…"

When they respond, the other party will often provide a longer answer than just "Yes" or "No." And when they disagree with the label, that is fine. You can always say, "I didn't say that was what it was; I only said it sounds that way."

Finally, the last thing about labeling is silence. Once you use a label, remain quiet, and listen. The emotions of human beings have two levels: the "presenting" behavior that is found above the surface, and the "underlying" feeling that is what drives the behavior.

When labeling, great negotiators focus on the underlying emotions. By labeling negatives, it diffuses them; if you label positives, it reinforces them.

Labeling is helpful because it removes angry confrontations as it makes a person internalize their feelings instead of continuing to act out.

The fastest and most efficient method of creating a quick working environment is to accept the negative and diffuse it.

Research has proven that the best way to handle negativity is to observe it without any judgment and reaction. Then you can consciously label every negative feeling and substitute it with positive, compassionate, and solution-based thoughts.

Put yourself in the other person's shoes. When you show concern for them, it will show that you are listening. And once they can see that you are listening, they can tell you something that you can use.

One of the reasons why the other party may fail to enter into a deal with you is usually very strong. In this case, you need to concentrate on eliminating barriers to reach an agreement.

Take the time to relax. Once you identify a barrier or mirror a person, wait for it to sink in. Don't be scared; the other party will value the silence. Identify the fears of the other party and then diffuse their power.

Create a list of the worst things that they can say about you and speak the words before the other person does. Since the following accusations may appear exaggerated when spoken aloud, by expressing them, it will motivate the other person to infer that the opposite is true.

Keep in mind that you are interacting with a person who wants to be understood and motivated. So you should focus on using labels to enhance and boost positive perceptions.

Learn "Yes"; Master "No"

Forcing a "yes" doesn't bring a negotiator nearer to a win; instead, it annoys the other party.

For great negotiators, "NO" offers an excellent chance for you and the other party to determine what you want by excluding what you don't want.

"No" is the beginning of a negotiation and not the end of it.

Good negotiators aim for "no" because they understand that is the point when the actual negotiation kicks in. "No" can generally mean:

- I am not ready to accept.

- You're causing me to feel very uncomfortable.

- I don't think I can afford it.

- I don't understand.

- I require extra information.

Ask for the solution-based type of questions: "What if this doesn't work for you?" "What do you need to ensure that it works? "It looks like there's something here that concerns you."

People may want to say, "No," straight away but don't; however, you should get them to say it early.

There are three types of "Yes":

- Counterfeit

- Confirmation

- Commitment

For the counterfeit "yes," the other party agrees to say "no" but finds that "yes" is the easiest route, and only wants to ensure that the conversation is on.

A confirmation "yes" in general is innocent, and a reflexive reply to a black or white question. Sometimes, it is used to set a trap, but in most cases, it is a simple affirmation without a promise of action.

Finally, there is the commitment "yes." This is the real deal, and it's the right agreement that results in the action "yes" at the table and a signature on the contract. This type of commitment is what you expect, but the three types look like the same, and so one has to learn to identify the one being used.

Whether you refer to it as "buy-in" or "engagement" or a different thing, great negotiators understand that their work is to guide the other party to discover their goal slowly.

While using all skills to build rapport, a connection, and an agreement with a counterpart is crucial, often this kind of relation is useless unless the other party feels they are accountable, if not responsible, for building the connection as well as the new ideas.

While the intensity can be different from individual to individual, you can be sure that everyone you come across is driven by two main urges: The need to feel safe and secure, and the need to be in control.

If you are attempting to sell something, avoid beginning with, "Do you have a few minutes to talk?" However, you can ask, "Is now a bad time to speak?" That way, you will receive, "Yes, it is a bad time" or "No, it's a good time."

"No" has many possibilities, such as:

- It will make it possible for the real challenges to be brought forth.

- It will protect people and provide them with a chance to correct ineffective decisions.

- It will slow things down so that people can readily embrace their decisions and agreements when they strike a deal.

- It will help people to feel emotionally comfortable, secure, and safe.

- It will move everyone's efforts forward.

Another means to force a "no" in a negotiation is by asking the other party what they don't want.

Even after you put in all your efforts, and the other party refuses to say, "No," you'll be dealing with people that are indecisive or have a hidden agenda.

By saying, "No," it will make the speaker feel secure and in control, and thus trigger it. And that is the reason why "Is now a bad time to speak?" is better than "Do you have a few minutes to talk?"

Sometimes, the only means for your counterpart to give you an ear and participate with you is to force them into a "no." It means deliberately mislabeling one of the emotions or asking ridiculous questions, such as, "It appears like you want the following project to fail"—this can only be responded to negatively.

When a prospective business party ignores you, you can decide to reach out to them using a clear and concise "NO" type of question that shows you are ready to walk away. For example, "Have you given up on the following project?" will work wonders.

Activate Two Words That Instantly Change Any Negotiation

Before you persuade the other party to see what you are attempting to accomplish, you need to tell them things that will make them say, "That's right."

"That's right" seems better than "Yes." By applying "that's right" in a conversation, it will generate breakthroughs.

You can also use a summary to activate "that's right." The building blocks of an excellent summary are a label combined using paraphrasing.

Transform Their Reality

The most critical word in a negotiation is "fair".

As you negotiate, you need to aim for a reputation of being fair. Your reputation will precede you. Allow it to preface you in a manner that creates success.

Understand the emotional drivers, and then you can build the benefits of any deal in a language that will rhyme.

To receive real leverage in a powerful negotiation, you need to convince the other party that they have something to lose when the deal succeeds. Below is how you can achieve that:

1. Trigger their emotions

To change the reality of the other party, you need to begin with an accusation audit to acknowledge all their fears. Begin by acknowledging their worries. Anchor their emotion and be ready for a loss. You will drive the other side's loss so that they jump at the idea to escape it.

2. Let the other person go first

Being the first one is never the best thing, especially when it comes to discussing the price. Instead, you should allow the other party to handle monetary negotiations. By allowing them to anchor, you might be lucky, but you also need to be careful. It is necessary to prepare yourself psychologically to handle the first offer. In case the other person is an expert, they may choose an extreme anchor to change your reality.

3. Determine a range

When you're confronted with naming your price, you should counter it by recalling a similar agreement which triggers your "ballpark". Rather than say, "You're worth $110,000," you can say, "People in this profession earn between $130,000 and $170,000." That will drive your point without causing the other party to jump into a defensive stance. And it will get him or her to think at a higher level.

4. Pivot to non-monetary terms

The best and simplest means to change the reality of the other party into your point of view is to pivot to non-monetary deals. Once you've anchored them high, you can bring your offer and appear reasonable by providing things that aren't important to you but could be vital to them. Or when the offer is low, you may request things that are more important to you than them.

5. When you say numbers, make sure to use odd ones

The numbers that finish with 0 will often appear like temporary placeholders that can be negotiated off. However, any figure that you mention rounded to say $47,234 seems as if you came up with it through a complex calculation.

6. Surprise with a gift

You can draw your counterpart into a mood of generosity by generating a deep anchor, and then, after their first rejection, provide them with an entirely different gift.

Build the Illusion of Control

When you walk into a store, instead of mentioning to the salesclerk whatever it is that you "need", you can choose to describe what you are looking for and ask questions. Once you have chosen what you want, rather than striking them, say that the price is a bit higher than what you had planned and request help using the best type of questions, such as "How am I supposed to do that?"

These types of questions have the potential to teach the other party what the problem is instead of generating conflict by telling them what the problem is.

You need to apply a calibrated question often, and there are a few things that you will find that you will employ at the start of each negotiation. For example, "What is the biggest problem that you face?"

Below are more examples that you can borrow:

- How can I assist in ensuring that this is better for us?
- What is it that brought us into the following situation?
- How would you like me to proceed?
- What's the objective?
- How am I supposed to do that?

By using these calibrated questions, it causes the other party to feel like they are in charge, but it is only you who is building the conversation.

Even with the best techniques and approaches, it is essential to control your emotions if you would like any chance of rising to the top.

The first and most important rule to maintain your emotional cool is to bite your tongue. Another simple idea is that when you are verbally abused, disarm your counterpart by asking a calibrated question.

When a person feels like they aren't in control, they apply what psychologists refer to as a "hostage mentality". That means that in times of conflict, they have to react to the lack of power by becoming very defensive.

Avoid questions that you can respond to with "yes" or short responses—these demand little thought and motivate the human desire for reciprocity; you will be required to give something back.

Include words such as "how" or "what" in the questions that you ask. By asking the other party for assistance, these questions will allow your counterpart to switch into an illusion of control and motivate them to talk longer, disclosing critical information.

Avoid asking questions that begin with "why" unless you want your counterpart to defend something that helps you. "Why" is usually an accusation used in any language.

Label your questions to refer your counterpart towards solving a given problem. That will help them to reveal their energy on developing a solution.

Guarantee Implementation

It is important for negotiators to become "decision architects". They need to dynamically develop both the nonverbal and verbal aspects of a negotiation to acquire both the permission and implementation.

A "yes" without "how" is nothing.

With enough "how" questions, it is possible to read and prepare the negotiating environment in a way that it will finally arrive at the answer you would like to hear.

The secret to "how" questions is to use gentle ways to say "no" and guide your counterpart to come up with a better solution. A gentle how/no creates collaboration and leaves the other party feeling respected.

Besides responding with a "no," the other main benefit of requesting "how?" is that it will force your counterpart to choose to consider and describe how a deal can be agreed upon.

By letting your counterparts mention implementation in their own words, you shall have carefully labeled "how" questions and convinced them that the last answer is their idea. This is important because people tend to dedicate a lot of effort into executing a solution when they believe it is theirs.

There are two significant questions you can request to push your counterparts to start thinking they are defining success in their way. For example, "How can I know that I'm on track?" and "How shall we address issues when we realize that we're off track?" When they respond, you can summarize their responses until you hear, "That's right." At this point, you will know that you have bought in.

Be worried of two clear signs that show your counterpart doesn't believe that the idea belongs to them. When they say, "You're right," it is usually a great indicator that they don't believe what is being discussed.

If you decide to push your execution, and you hear something like, "I'll try," just know that it means, "I plan to fail."

And when you hear none of the above, switch back with a calibrated "how" question until they determine the terms of a successful execution using their voice.

Next, follow up by summarizing what they have said to get a "that's right."

You need to be aware of "level II" players. This includes parties that aren't directly involved but can assist in implementing agreements they prefer and blocking the ones they don't.

Below you will find the tools, tactics, and methods for applying subtle verbal and nonverbal types of communication to learn and change the mental state of your counterpart.

• The 7-38-55 percent rule

According to this rule, only 77% of a message contains words while 38% originates from the tone of voice and 55% comes from the body language and face of the speaker.

Pay attention to body language and tone to ensure that they go hand in hand with the literal meaning of the words. If they don't, it's likely that the speaker isn't convinced or is lying.

Whenever the tone or body language of a person doesn't match their words, use labels to identify the origin of the incongruence.

Identify the incongruence and gently handle it with the other party without disrespecting them.

• The rule of three

The rule of three tries to persuade the other party to agree to the same thing three times in the same conversation.

The first time they give you a commitment is marked as No 1. For No. 2, you can label or summarize what they said for them to respond, "That's right." And the third time you can calibrate it using "how" or "what" for them to describe what constitutes success. It could be something like, "What can we do if we're off track?"

The three times can also take the form of the calibrated question three times.

How to get the other party to bid against themselves

The best approach to making the other party reduce their demands is by saying "NO" and applying "how" questions. These are indirect methods of saying "no" that can't shut down your counterpart.

The first step is to use the old standby: "How am I supposed to perform that?" You need to deliver it respectfully so that it turns into a request for assistance. A correct delivery causes the other party to take part in your dilemma and come up with a better offer.

Next, some examples of "Your offer is sincere; however, I'm sorry, but that doesn't work for me" is a smart way to say "No."

This well-tested reply avoids creating a counteroffer, and the application of the term "generous" causes your counterpart to stick to the word. The "I'm sorry" also tends to soften the "No" and establish empathy.

You can then follow it up with something like, "I'm sorry, but I'm afraid I just can't do that," which does a good job. By displaying the inability to perform, it can generate the other side's empathy.

If you have to go further, then "No" is the last and most direct way. Verbally, you need to deliver it with a downward inflection and a tone of respect, so not a "NO!"

Bargain hard

When you feel you are being "pushed against a wall", you can divert the conversation to non-monetary issues that will make the final price work. You can do this by speaking in a persuasive tone: "Let's put price off to the side for now and discuss what would make this a better deal." Or "What else can you offer to make that a better price for me?"

When the negotiation is far from reaching a solution, you need to shake things up and push your counterpart away from a rigid mindset. When you are about to flip a dubious colleague to your direction, ask them, "Why would you do that?" but in a manner that favors you.

If you want to win a client from a particular competitor, you could say, "Why would you do business with me? Why would you think of changing your current supplier?" The "why" question persuades the counterpart to consider working with you.

Using the first-person singular pronoun is a great way to define a boundary without getting into an altercation. When you say, "I'm sorry, that doesn't work for me," the term "I" strategically concentrates your counterpart's attention onto you to the extent that you make a point.

If you want to challenge unproductive statements from your counterpart, you can say, "I feel _when_ because_," and that requires a timeout from the other person.

How to Negotiate: Essential Real Estate Negotiation Tips

Some people think that the skills they use to negotiate little deals are different from the skills needed to buy big-ticket items, such as real estate, companies, and cars.

While it is possible for a person to spend their whole life trying to master the technique of negotiation, learning some negotiation strategies can place you far ahead of your competitors and help you overcome the times when you encounter an unmotivated seller or a savvy buyer.

In summary, when going through a negotiation process, consider the following issues before you close the deal. They are great real estate negotiation tips for sellers and buyers:

> • Often, there are options and other things to consider. Don't agree on a poor deal when you know that there's a better one.

• Research is important. Stay familiar with the property and all the features of the neighborhood. You can learn from the seller, but you could discover something that may increase the value of the property, so you should conduct your own investigation. The more you know, the better you become.

• Be likable. Enter into negotiations in a manner that doesn't disrespect the other party. Make sure that you show respect and be fair. The odds are high that the other party may be cooperative and ready to consider your needs. This may also include discussing the terms that the other person wants and being thoughtful of their desires. Keep in mind the adage, "What goes around, comes around." Also, it is necessary to find a similarity, such as heritage, sports, or anything else that will help cement the friendship.

• Compare numbers with different parties, such as real estate agents, appraisers, and experienced friends who own property. Some appraisers will offer you a value that has an extension of six months.

• Don't disclose information that you consider secretive, such as the value of the property and future ideas.

• Know your goal and what you want to afford. Also, this is related to determining your plans and goals. The point is to be realistic and patient.

Purchasing an investment property is one of the most significant steps towards becoming a successful rental property investor or expanding your rental investment business. With the right negotiating power, you will make the best decision and grab an investment property. The tips discussed above will be of great help in striking an agreement on the price of a property and the rest of the terms for purchasing a new income rental property.

Chapter 7: The Secrets of Rental Property Investing and Management

Picking the Right Plan

A rental property is a significant type of investment, and with any investment, there is some risk involved. That is why you need to have an insurance plan that will protect your business. In other words, an insurance plan will secure your assets so that you can avoid any stress. However, finding the right program can be very difficult when you don't have enough information and knowledge.

This book has made everything easy for you by compiling information that you need to be aware of when choosing an insurance plan for your rental property. With a foundation of the basics, you can make a smart decision and feel confident about going forward:

1. Difference between homeowners insurance and landlord insurance

You'll need something more besides the existing homeowner's policy that protects your rental property. Although the insurance for homeowners and landlords covers damages, the landlord insurance offers greater security. For example, it covers any loss of income that you may experience during a repair.

The landlord insurance policy also has the liability coverage for any legal issues that may emerge from an injury on your property. So, there's nothing to worry about over a slip and a fall.

Although the above features of landlord insurance look attractive, there are some costs. On average, you may have to pay between 10-20% more compared to homeowners insurance premiums, although the last calculation depends on the type of dwelling policy you choose to buy.

2. The different types of dwelling policies

You'll need to define your dwelling policy based on several factors, but the most important is the size of your budget. If you have enough money, go for a comprehensive policy, but if not, you can pick an affordable option. Below are the three types of plans available:

- DP-1 Policy. It includes primary coverage of risks, such as theft.

- Dp-2 Policy. It includes moderate coverage, which includes additional risks, such as fire and damage.

- Dp-3 policy. It is detailed and includes all the potential perils.

In most cases, a Dp-3 policy is the best option. Why? It pays a complete replacement of costs on a claim rather than actual cash value. For example, if you have an old property that is subject to severe damage, you'll receive just a fraction of the money.

3. Understand the importance of renter's insurance.

You can protect your rental property, but you'll still be at risk if the tenants are yet to buy the renter's insurance. They can hold you accountable if they happen to incur losses to their possessions, and this can extend into a lawsuit that you could have avoided beforehand.

To avoid any unnecessary disputes, you should compel all your tenants to buy renter's insurance. It's a tiny detail that can save you a significant sum of money if something bad were to happen. It is strongly advised that, as a rental property investor, you take this precaution and secure your wallet.

Which policy to buy?

The type of policy to buy depends on your unique situation. Some landlords go for a Dp-2 policy; others don't feel comfortable without a DP. Whichever plan you choose, you should get in touch with a professional and discuss the little details of what you want, avoiding any worries that you may have about a given policy.

Picking the Right Members of Your Rental Property Investing Team

Building a rental property investing group is critical to realizing success in the real estate business. The best real estate investors know the real value that a team brings to the business. It is just hard to be everywhere or even do everything on your own. This is the time when your real estate team comes into play.

Who are they?

A rental property investing team is a group of professionals that work closely with you before, during, and even after buying a rental property. The role of this team is to help you with sourcing deals, running the due diligence process, financing, and assisting in the general management of the investment.

As you continue to build your rental property portfolio, having a professional team to work with can save you valuable time and money. The secret to making a successful team is to look for reliable individuals. Come up with a solid group of experts that you can turn to for any assistance.

Why should you have a rental property investing team?

A complete rental property investing guide should mention the significance of building a well-grounded rental property investing team. Everyone has different goals and ambitions in real estate, but whatever goals you have, you stand a significant chance of realizing them when you have a solid team. It is essential to look at your real estate members as business partners who are there to help you reach your goal in rental property investing.

Key members of a real estate investing team:

- Real estate agent
- Spouse
- Lawyer
- Lenders
- Insurance agent
- Bookkeeper
- Contractors

When should you build your investment team?

It is essential to start building your rental property investment team as soon as possible. Don't wait until you own ten rental properties. Remember: the value of your team continues to double as you establish your professional relationships. These members are your teammates, and having these key people at the beginning can help you realize massive success faster. Your rental property investment team can be helpful during the due diligence purchasing period.

Where can you find these members?

There are many different places where you can look for team members, but the top place to start is by asking other rental property investors. You can find real estate investors by attending local real estate meetups, real estate groups on Facebook, and real estate forums. Real estate investors like to work closely with rental property investing team members. As you continue to build your team, you should ask your members to tell you whether they know of some real estate investor friends in their network.

How to manage your rental like a pro?

While real estate is also considered a passive income method, this is not a type of business that you will set and forget, and where you sit back and expect money to roll in. Once you identify a rental property to purchase, there are many different tasks that you need to do to ensure that you fulfill your goal.

Whether you want to manage real estate for yourself or you have been hired as a property manager, you will want to use a strategy that will generate income at the end of every month. If you have ever asked yourself, "Can I manage my rental property?" and you are looking for ways to manage your rental property, then this section is for you.

Major responsibilities of managing a rental property

It is crucial that you know the three fundamental areas of rental property investment that need to be controlled:

- Managing tenants
- Managing the property
- Handling the finances

Tenants play a crucial role in any rental investment, and spending the time to screen and choose great tenants will provide you with the highest odds of achieving success.

Rental Property Management Secrets

Managing Tenants

Great management of tenants requires a person to have excellent people skills, especially when it involves addressing complaints brought up by tenants. Learning the most common complaints and how to be proactive in fixing them will increase the rate of tenants staying in your property. By following up with a tenant after you have made some repairs, be it pest invasion or water leakages, demonstrates that you are very caring and concerned about their stay. Even when the complaint comes from an unknown source, being respectful and responding fashionably increases the chances of tenants remaining in your property. The best way to ensure that tenants are always okay is to perform regular property inspections. This way, you will notice areas that need repair and prevent complaints from tenants.

The landlord's first concern with new tenants is non-payment of rent. A tenant who doesn't pay rent on time can cause a major hassle. Landlords can take several measures to ensure that these problems don't happen by using rent reminders and penalties for delays. Choosing to use online rent payments is another excellent way to offer tenants convenient ways to pay rent on time.

If you prevent costly evictions, then your profit from the rental investment will be high. Besides the late payments, there could be other reasons, such as threats to the security of your property that would trigger eviction. If you have to conduct the eviction process, make sure that you do it according to the rules in your state. Typically, you can prevent eviction from happening by screening your tenants to ensure that you only let in high-quality tenants.

Another critical factor is the tenant turnover; this factor can eat into your profits very fast. Although tenant turnover is a natural feature of renting, and may even grant you the chance to charge more rent to the tenant moving in, it can also consume your profits if it happens regularly. The only sure way to ensure that you maintain your benefits from your rental property is to make your tenants happy. Most of these things are pretty simple, such as responding to calls that require you to perform repairs and adding some features that will attract or make your current tenants want to continue to stay.

Doing some strategic upgrades may also make a house appear like a home and encourage tenants to stay longer. When handling tenants, you must ensure that you adhere strictly to the landlord-tenant rules. It should include the federal Fair Housing Act and other local regulations. Refunding security deposits, choosing tenants, and putting up a notice before entering are all processes that the landlord-tenant law requires. It is crucial that you learn about this to ensure that you optimize your management responsibilities.

Property Maintenance

As a landlord, you have a legal mandate to secure your property and ensure that it is safe to stay in. One thing that you will struggle with is finding good tenants if maintenance is a problem. However, it is more cost effective to perform regular repairs and maintain the property than having to wait until an emergency arises. One of the main risks of becoming a landlord is handling massive maintenance problems that can be expensive and that your insurance may not cover.

Some property maintenance has to be done every year so that you don't end up with an emergency. Whether there is an issue or not, it is good to replace the supply hoses and drain lines on a dishwasher and washing machine. If you have an old property, it could be time to look for a plumber to come in and replace water valves and sink faucets. By doing the following repairs, you will reduce the risk of water-related issues down the line.

Remodeling your property can ensure that your rental remains profitable, and again, you could save money repairing before doing a complete replacement. For example, you will save some costs cleaning a carpet before buying new carpets.

Hiring a Property Manager

The decision of whether to hire a property manager or not depends on a few unique factors. Those outside the state may have to involve a third party to deal with the daily operations of rental property investment. Additionally, if you live near your rental property, you can as well hire a property manager to help you with the management of the property. Sometimes, you may not have the time to commit to managing the property, or you don't want to be interrupted early in the morning for emergencies. Even when you hire a property manager to help manage your property, it doesn't mean that you have no control over the daily operations that take place in your rental. A good property manager can perform most of the management responsibilities, turning your rental into a real passive income investment. If you are going to hire a property manager, then you must ensure that you're on the same page when it comes to selecting a tenant. Since most property managers may not have the same desire as a landlord, they may not deal with problems in the same way.

Secrets to Successful Property Investment

The idea of earning millions through investing in real estate is one that is attracting many investors. Here is a compilation of secrets to boost your success in real estate investment:

Realize the commitments on your time

Of course, rental property investment requires some capital to start, but if you choose to rent your property, you need to be prepared to face the bad, useful, and ugly sides of this choice. There is a great difference between a homeowner and a landlord. It is perhaps one of the most significant factors that you'll need to decide when buying a property to rent rather than to live in. Being a landlord isn't that hard, but there is a lot of work. No matter whether you are dealing with a tenant directly or a rental property management company, you'll still receive some emergency calls about water leakages or unexpected costs to fix a faulty washing machine. So, before you enter the world of rental property investment, be sure to commit what is required to ensure that the venture is successful.

Draw your investment strategy

Are you interested in a fix-and-flip property to make a profit? Or do you want to purchase a property and rent? How much income do you require to cover mortgage bills and fundamental expenses? What is the projected capital growth of the property? Do you have an exit strategy? If you can answer these questions, then you will know how best to achieve your goals. You can be a very ambitious investor wanting to resign full-time work and quickly build a portfolio to act as your primary source of income, or you could be a homeowner wanting to make some additional income through renting out a property. Once you have written down your reasons for investing and your goals, then your initial investment strategy can begin.

Always look for properties and potential places

Properties that demand many repairs can be a big turnoff to investors, as it brings up the issue of time and capital before it is ready to let. While a turnkey property can easily attract tenants, it does not have the same ability to generate high profit. A well-built and furnished property will not only produce a higher profit, but the value of the property will also increase. That means that you stand a greater chance of walking away with a huge income if you decide to sell the property. However, for this to happen, the location is also important. There are lovely houses that lie empty because the location is undesirable. The secret is to research the market and act fast when the right opportunity presents itself.

Four Rental Property Investment Sins That Will Ruin Your Investment

1. Coming up with your rental rates

You could be asking, "What is so hard about determining rental rates?"

What you need to do is look for a newspaper or jump on Craigslist and pick a number, right? Also, you're bright enough to perform some basic math and know that when your mortgage payment is about $800/month, then you need an extra buck to cover expenses.

But how much extra do you need to cover for expenses?

Well, anything over $1 goes into your account. So, you want as much as you can get, but at the same time not chase away your tenants. Plus, you've already spent something on repair and improvements. That's got to be more than a few bucks.

That causes you to start thinking about all the work you've done. When you compute and sum up everything, you now realize it is time to be paid back. So, quickly, the idea of rent shoots up in your mind. Then, right as you are about to post your advertisement with a hiked rental rate, you notice places for rent in your area that cause you to begin rubbing your neck. You ask yourself how a beautiful place like that can have cheap rent?

Why trusting your gut to increase rental rates reduces your profits

Humans are emotional creatures, and thus, they become passionate about things that they invest their money in. You convince yourself that a person is going to love the way you've decorated the garden, so when deciding the rental rates, it can be difficult to lower that.

The same applies to your imported cupboards, tiles, and anything else that you did to improve the appearance of your place. Although these are all great things to do, when you become emotionally invested in the value of the improvement, it is the sure way to harm your ability to make the right decisions about the amount of rent to charge. That is like trying to help someone in trouble who didn't even ask for your help—you'll feel disappointed when they don't recognize all the support you rendered to them.

Does this mean that you don't need to make your rental property attractive? No. You only need someone to assist you in seeing how the market appreciates all your efforts and improvements. But you can't just decide to "ballpark" your rental rates from newspapers and Craigslist.

How to look for rental comps that value your property's unique changes and assets

There are different types of online websites and tools that you can turn to in order to receive rental comps in a given market. Some charge a membership fee per month; others charge a fixed fee for reports. Although this is a huge improvement over listening to your gut and using Craigslist, it has its cons.

For newbies, most of the comp sites only focus on significant sites. So, if your property is located in a rural place, you'll have to use grassroot techniques. Another problem is that they have no methods to measure the actual value of your improvements.

That's where you need to look for a professional property management company. They will run an in-depth market study to determine the price of your property. Besides that, they will evaluate your investments and create a profitable strategy for your particular market conditions.

Are these property management companies expensive?

Hardly. According to a report from Census Bureau, rental owners must deduct over "20% of their rental income" to handle maintenance, then 6-10% is charged by a property management company.

So, you can see why you can't risk trusting your gut about rental rates.

Regardless of whether you combine local tools, partner with a property management company, or use comp sites, you cannot risk trusting your gut feeling. Why? If you quote wrong or a lower rate to entice tenants, you'll always pay for it in the long run. That is why you should seek objective assistance when you want to set your rental rates.

2. Searching for rent checks

You're a nice person, and this is something that you find difficult to overcome. Now, do you stop being nice and become a heartless cheapskate to be effective? Of course not.

However, many landlords and property owners who find it hard to make profits think that they're kind to let payments on security deposits be late, which then they chase for months. And their soft hearts start to be taken advantage of every month with many excuses about expensive daycare or some other story.

Why you need an emotionless strategy to collect rent?

Remember that you're running a business in which cash flow is the main deal. When you receive rent late, then your mortgage is likely late. In other words, your bank is going to charge you a certain fee. Do you notice how your bank doesn't care regardless of how valid your excuse for late payments is? Just keep being late, and they'll come for their property.

So you need to develop the same mindset

Your bank has a strategy and an emotionless system. Once you're late by a day, the computer automatically computes that. At the same time, a penalty is set immediately one minute past your grace period. The only method to get free and maintain your property is to pay for it. You can choose to turn a blind eye on their phone calls, letters, and automated emails, and they will resort to a pre-planned action like seizing your house.

You may consider this action as being cold-hearted, but it's precisely what you need to have. The same way you signed on paper before owning the house, your tenants must sign off on what should be done when they are late in rent payments.

Typically, this is often a fee of $50-60, with additional charges for every late day after that. But you don't sit back and wait for them to pay. If you're a profit-minded landlord, you'll begin the eviction process immediately after the grace period. There's nothing wrong with it. If they happen to pay, the eviction process is canceled.

With today's modern technology, creating an effective rent collection system is as easy as 1-2-3

If paper and pencil are the systems that you use to receive rent, then you're losing profits. The modern changes in technology have come with endless software systems that make it easy to collect your rent on time.

A "foolproof" rent collection method has many moving parts. First, here's how you want to collect the rent. There are legal features of what you can charge and when you can begin the eviction process. That means that you must have an efficient team and system in place—because most landlords, even with their best intentions, learn about their legal rights only after being summoned different times in court.

The hard truth about the rental collection

If you fail to install a reliable and accurate system that includes the laws to collect rents, then you'll be phased out of the business.

Whether you choose to design your system or use a rental investor's network, you can eliminate the hassle and drama of collecting rent and secure your investment's most important asset.

3. Anemic Marketing

Your property isn't the only property for rent around your community, so you'll have to be ready to compete for attention from tenants. If your marketing strategy is to post an advertisement on Craigslist anytime there's a vacancy then you're in trouble.

This reactive technique is harmful to your nerves and will result in stupid mistakes.

Why should you always think like a marketer?

Successful rental property owners often think ahead. This also means they do future marketing. They keep thinking about the things that make their property and community unique. They look for ways to change the market by making improvements and polishing the outside appearance.

They like to rely on insights mined from tenants' surveys and market studies to learn the kind of improvements that are likely to match with increased rents. They know what high-quality tenants consider and hope to attract and pass that message in every ad, flyer, and brochure they create.

Even after doing this, they don't feel satisfied that this will attract stellar tenants to their property. So, they decide to study and test new ads and marketing funnels. They refine their ads based on one thing: results.

It's hard to explain everything about how to market, how to distinguish your property in ads, and how to get your property before the eyes of your prospective tenants in this section.

But what we can tell you is how effective marketing can attract many tenants

Depending on how your property is when a tenant vacates, it may require one-two weeks to prepare a house before the next person moves in. In other words, your property may lie idle for weeks. Vacancies are dangerous because they can wipe out a whole year's profit or more.

If you have multiple units, it is hard for all the units to be fully occupied. That is why you're advised to watch out for who is about to leave.

If you want your property to be occupied fully and generate enough profit, you need to hire a person to help you market it. Luckily, you can look for people to assist you. No need for an ad agency, but you can choose to hire marketers from different platforms online. But still, you will need to supervise and pay for specific ads.

4. Renting to the wrong persons

If you have a rental property, it's just a matter of time before you get in touch with a "professional tenant". These are tenants who think that by owning the property, you need to allow them rent-free living.

Your application steps are intended to eliminate these kinds of people. However, the professional tenant will prey on you with loose rental agreements and shoddy move-in steps. That is what gives them the power in court to show the judge that you're a "slumlord".

How can you avoid costly and embarrassing court battles with "professional tenants"?

The way to avoid this kind of battle is to screen each applicant. As long as they are over eighteen years old, they have to be grilled; it doesn't matter whether you know them or not. You also need to have an effective process for phone and personal screenings so that you can identify them before you waste your time.

Let every applicant fill out a form. They should also sign documents to let you extract credit reports and contact current and previous employers and landlords if they show some resistance.

Reach out to every employer and landlord contact that is given. Just making a phone call alone is not enough, and you should consider asking questions.

Good landlords reject many people before they accept someone, and the reason is that they have a well-defined standard of the type of tenant they want. If you don't get your screening process correctly, then you could waste time and money in court. If you can get this right, it will be easy for you to defend yourself in court.

Although you can do all of the screening process and looking for tenants yourself, know that an online screening tool is still not enough.

You must conduct a complete process from the first response to your ad until when you give them the keys. Don't skip the attorney because they will ensure that your legal work is in order in case a professional tenant emerges.

There's a shortcut to avoid doing all this yourself, and that is to hire a property management company. They are experienced at looking for good tenants and will handle all the details.

Exit Strategies and Exchanges

1. Hold forever

For all the talk related to flipping properties for profit and fun, rental property investment focuses on becoming wealthy slowly. Purchasing a property that you can hold on to for a good number of years is better and, in many situations, it is an easy strategy compared to dealing with a fast flip. Going with this slower technique can be different from what you see on TV, but it can be helpful when you need to establish a continuous income to enhance the finances of your family.

Planning an exit strategy

Purchasing a rental investment property to hold on to has a different meaning to different people. One way involves buying a property and keeping it forever. For other people, it means purchasing a property and holding it for around ten years and then selling it for a higher price. Your exit plan will tell you how you can buy and control the property, so you need to determine the program before you can get started. Just make sure that you include potential tax strategies to reduce the bill when you sell.

2. Seller financing deals

It is an option to use traditional financing when trying to get a mortgage. With the following conditions, seller financing will assist a person to receive an alternative type of credit. Sellers can then involve a certain number of buyers who don't qualify for a traditional mortgage, and since the seller is financing the sale, the property may have a higher return.

A bank isn't involved directly in a seller-financed sale. Both the buyer and seller make plans for themselves. They come up with a note that defines the interest rate, sets the payment dates, and the results—just in case the buyer decides to default.

When only two players are taking part in seller finance, it can be quick and cheaper than customarily selling a home.

The closing costs for a seller-financed sale are lower since a bank is not involved. When the bank doesn't participate, the transaction will minimize the values of the mortgage and the origination of the fee. The seller financing sale only runs for a short term that could be only five years, with a "balloon payment" at the end of the period. The hope is that the buyer will refinance the loan using a traditional lender.

Conclusion

Congratulations on making it to the end of Rental Property Investing: Unlock the Secrets of Real Estate Investing and Management, Including Tips on Negotiation and Finding Investment Properties that Will Give You Passive Long-term Income. It should have been informative and provided you with all of the tools you need to achieve your goals.

Real estate investment does not have a map, and the road to riches is not straight. You will have to climb the mountains and hills. That said, there are things that you can do and follow to put yourself on the right path and ensure that you have the best chances for success. Listening to real estate investors and professionals is a great place to start. Besides, you can combine it with the tips and secrets discussed in this book to ensure that you manage your investment in the best way possible.

Now all that is left for you to do is spring forward, grab your future, and enjoy your success. You have the drive, the tools, and the passion!

Finally, if you found this book useful in any way, a review on Amazon is always appreciated.

www.ingramcontent.com/pod-product-compliance
Lightning Source LLC
Chambersburg PA
CBHW030530210326
41597CB00014B/1095